Welfarewell

by Cat Delaney

A SAMUEL FRENCH ACTING EDITION

SAMUEL FRENCH

FOUNDED 1830

NEW YORK HOLLYWOOD LONDON TORONTO

SAMUELFRENCH.COM

ISBN 978-0-573-69834-7   Printed in U.S.A.   #29609

MUSIC USE NOTE

Licensees are solely responsible for obtaining formal written permission from copyright owners to use copyrighted music in the performance of this play and are strongly cautioned to do so. If no such permission is obtained by the licensee, then the licensee must use only original music that the licensee owns and controls. Licensees are solely responsible and liable for all music clearances and shall indemnify the copyright owners of the play and their licensing agent, Samuel French, Inc., against any costs, expenses, losses and liabilities arising from the use of music by licensees.

IMPORTANT BILLING AND CREDIT REQUIREMENTS

All producers of *WELFAREWELL must* give credit to the Author of the Play in all programs distributed in connection with performances of the Play, and in all instances in which the title of the Play appears for the purposes of advertising, publicizing or otherwise exploiting the Play and/or a production. The name of the Author *must* appear on a separate line on which no other name appears, immediately following the title and *must* appear in size of type not less than fifty percent of the size of the title type.

In addition the following credit *must* be given in all programs and publicity information distributed in association with this piece:

Winner of the Samuel French Canadian Playwriting Competition

WELFAREWELL was selected for a staged reading at the Women Playwrights International conference in Mumbai, India, November 1-7, 2009. The playwright gave a reading, playing all roles, of Act I, Scene 5, at The Space, Halifax, Nova Scotia, Canada, February 20, 2009.

WELFAREWELL was the winner of the 2009 Samuel French Canadian Playwriting Competition.

CHARACTERS

ESMERELDA QUIPP – 80, a former actress, pensioner. Esmerelda has a refined "stage" English accent.

H.B. (HONEY BUNCH) HACKETT – 35, police officer

VAL – 30, a film actress, posing as a hooker (real name is Rosanna Palermo)

PENELOPE FARTHINGALE – 45, a hard-drinking hooker, past her best-before date, and lacking a pension plan

DOTTIE RAMSBOTTOM – 50, a compulsive shoplifter

ALFRED DAVID – 30, lawyer; a weary public defender

JENNIFER DOER – 25, a naïve social worker/do-gooder

GLADYS SYMMINGTON-BUKOVITCH – 55, a rich woman who shot her husband, but he failed to die

JUDGE JULIUS – 55, a crusty, caring female

MILDRED MCGONIGLE – 60-ish, a bank customer

LANDLORD – 40, a beer-bellied bully

Three **BANK TELLERS** and one **BANK CUSTOMER**

A **CHEF**

Radio Voices

KING LEAR, EDGAR, ANNOUNCER, CORDELIA, GLOUSTER
(all male voices can be read by the male actor with different inflections; **CORDELIA** should be read the actor playing **VAL**)

Doubling for Actors

Female #1: **ESMERELDA QUIPP**

Female #2: **H.B. HACKETT; BANK CUSTOMER**

Female #3: **VAL/ROSANNA PALERMO; BANK TELLER**

Female #4: **PENELOPE FARTHINGALE; BANK TELLER**

Female #5: **DOTTIE RAMSBOTTOM; MILDRED MCGONIGLE**

Female #6: **JENNIFER DOER; BANK TELLER**

Female #7: **GLADYS SYMMINGTON-BUKOVITCH; JUDGE JULIUS**

Male #1: **ALFRED DAVID; LANDLORD; CHEF**

SCENE BREAKDOWN

Act One

Scene 1: Esmerelda's One-room Basement Flat
Scene 2: The Yard Outside Esmerelda's Flat
Scene 3: The Night Desk in a Police Station
Scene 4: The Front Desk of the Police Station
Scene 5: A Bank
Scene 6: The Holding Cell in the Police Station Jail
Scene 7: The Private Meeting Room (known as the "Torture Chamber")
Scene 8: The Holding Cell in the Police Station Jail

Act Two

Scene 1: The Alleyway Behind a Restaurant
Scene 2: Another Bank
Scene 3: The Holding Cell in the Police Station Jail
Scene 4: The Private Meeting Room (known as the "Torture Chamber")
Scene 5: The Holding Cell in the Police Station Jail
Scene 6: The Night Desk in the Police Station
Scene 7: A Courtroom
Scene 8: The Holding Cell in the Police Station Jail

ACT I

Scene One
Esmerelda's One-room Basement Flat

(It's winter; the flat is cold. **ESMERELDA,** *wrapped in a shawl and walking with a cane, is in her kitchen, listening to the radio as she struggles with arthritic hands and a manual can-opener on a tin of cat food. An audio of Shakespeare's "King Lear" plays on the radio, with sound effects.)*

EDGAR. *(on radio)* What, in ill thoughts again? Men must their going hence, even as their coming hither: Ripeness is all – Come on.

ESMERELDA. *(over* **GLOUSTER***)* Ripeness, indeed. Falling off the flipping vine!

GLOUSTER. *(under* **ESMERELDA***)* And that's true too.

ANNOUNCER. *(on radio)* Exuent.

ESMERELDA. Merlin; here, puss-puss.

ANNOUNCER. *(on radio)* Act five, scene three. The British Camp near Dover. Entering, in conquest with drum and colours, comes Edmund with Lear and Cordelia as his prisoners, along with officers and soldiers.

ESMERELDA. Prisoners. Alas. Aren't we all?

EDMUND. *(on radio)* Some officers take them away: good guard, until their greater pleasures first be known that are to censure them.

CORDELIA *(on radio)* **& ESMERELDA.** We are not the first who, with best meaning have incurr'd the worst. For thee, oppressed king, I am cast down; myself could else out-frown false fortune's frown. – Should we not see these daughters and these sisters?

LEAR. *(on radio)* No, no, no, no! Come, let's away to prison: we two alone will sing like birds i' the cage...

(The lights flicker briefly and go out.)

ESMERELDA. What next, I ask you.

(There is a long pause filled with general noises before **ESMERELDA** *strikes a match and lights candles.* **ESMERELDA** *picks up the telephone receiver and pauses.)*

ESMERELDA. No point whatsoever in ringing the electric company, is there Merlin?

*(***ESMERELDA*** *replaces the receiver on the rocker.)*

ESMERELDA. Given that the telephone is now relegated to the status of a mere ornament... Merlin?

*(***ESMERELDA*** *scoops part of the tin of cat food into a small dish and the rest onto a slice of bread.)*

ESMERELDA. This is the sole advantage of not being able to see very well. If the bread has mould, I shan't know until I feel like I've just had a swig of beer.

*(***ESMERELDA*** *eats the bread.)*

ESMERELDA. Ghastly. How do you stand this stuff, puss-puss?

*(***ESMERELDA*** *raises a glass of tap water and squints to see the glass and contents.)*

ESMERELDA. No apparent fish, seaweed or metal shavings.

*(***ESMERELDA*** *downs a handful of pills with the glass of water.)*

ESMERELDA. Dessert prescription. What I'd give for just one perfect petits-fours. A smidgen of sachertorte. A dollop of gooseberry fool.

*(***ESMERELDA*** *drinks the rest of the water like it is something sweet and delicious, closes her eyes and enjoys the imaginary taste. The moment is soon gone...)*

ESMERELDA. No heat, no electricity. Spring is two months away. What ever shall we do, puss-puss?

(**ESMERELDA** *carries the dish toward the fireplace, which has no wood, never mind not being aflame, where Merlin's basket and blanket are situated.*)

ESMERELDA. Din-dins, Merlin. Merlin? Say meow to Mummy, little laddie. Merlin?

(**ESMERELDA** *reaches down to touch her cat, but he is dead; she collapses into tears.*)

ESMERELDA. Oh, Merlin! You were all I had left.

(**ESMERELDA** *sobs, adding a little over-drama.*)

ESMERELDA. I've no reason to carry on! Oh, Merlin!

(**ESMERELDA** *sobs for a while and then pauses, sniffling.*)

ESMERELDA. And what I am to do with you now, my Merlin? No sense going to the vet. And I can't put you with Guinevere and Arthur, not until…

(**ESMERELDA** *lovingly touches two urns on the mantel.*)

ESMERELDA. I'd always thought we'd be together one day, the four of us. One great heap of ashes. But then, who would there be to scatter us? All our friends are dead, too. Like you, my beloved puss-puss. And like me. This is hardly living; I'm merely hanging about, waiting to die.
"The miserable have no other medicine, but only hope; I have hope to live and am prepar'd to die."
Fat lot Shakespeare knew about death. Writers romanticize the hell out of everything.

(**ESMERELDA**, *weeping, tucks the cat into an old tea towel, and then wraps him in a plastic grocery bag, tying it closed.*)

ESMERELDA. How awfully undignified. For a regal magician like you. Perhaps I can bury you in the yard, and then when I amass a little money, I'll have you properly cremated. I've failed you, Merlin, failed us both.

(With great difficulty, unsteady without her cane,
ESMERELDA *tugs on an old coat, and then carries the*
cat's body to the door, marching slowly as though she
were pallbearer to a king; she opens the door and exits.)

Scene Two
The Yard Outside Esmerelda's Flat

(ESMERELDA, using a garden trowel, digs.)

ESMERELDA. My dear boy, you wouldn't mind awfully if I have that last bit of tuna supper in sauce, would you?

(ESMERELDA finds a garden spade and begins to dig in earnest.)

ESMERELDA. Everything sounds better in French. Thon au sauce. Poulet et dinde.

(The LANDLORD enters; he's not happy.)

ESMERELDA. Fricassee du landlord.

LANDLORD. What the hell you doing?

ESMERELDA. Good afternoon. I'm burying Merlin, my cat.

LANDLORD. Ain't legal to bury pets in yards! Check the damn by-laws.

ESMERELDA. I'd prefer to cremate him, as per his last wishes.

LANDLORD. Last whiskers?

ESMERELDA. Wishes. Last wishes. For instance, your last wish might be to be blown apart by an ouzi. Excuse me; you're standing where I need to dig.

LANDLORD. Oh, I get it.

ESMERELDA. Excellent good news, my lord. Are you in my way, perchance?

(The LANDLORD steps out of the way and ESMERELDA digs.)

LANDLORD. Wait a sec! Cats don't got no will.

ESMERELDA. Evidently you've never had a cat.

LANDLORD. Had some up at the old barn when I was a kid. They all got smoked out when the barn went on fire one night.

ESMERELDA. Perchance, do you happen to have a bit of spare firewood?

LANDLORD. You'd burn the damn thing in your fireplace?

ESMERELDA. He's not a damn thing, he's... Was a cat. My cat. Kindly show some respect.

LANDLORD. Firstly, you can't bury nobody when the ground's frozen. Secondly, you can't bury that damn thing in my damn yard.

ESMERELDA. Incorrect. That would be first, not firstly, and I can bury anybody, as nobody will not be buried.

LANDLORD. And your rent's two weeks overdue.

ESMERELDA. Correction: three weeks. You see, I had a choice. Rent or food. Given that I should die if I have no food to eat, I selected to purchase food; that way there's a fighting chance I'll actually be alive to pay the rent.

LANDLORD. Hey, it's dark down there.

ESMERELDA. It's a cellar.

LANDLORD. Power cut off again?

ESMERELDA. Brilliant deduction, Einstein. If it was still on, I could store Merlin in the freezer until spring. *(pauses)* Now, there's a jolly little thought! You have that very large chest freezer in the storage room...

LANDLORD. No way! There's food in there. I'm calling the cops. You're in default and this ain't legal.

ESMERELDA. Isn't legal; your grammar is the crime here!

LANDLORD. So, sue me!

ESMERELDA. And I don't give a toss that it's not legal!

LANDLORD. A toss? Toss the damn thing in the river!

*(The **LANDLORD** tries to grab the cat's corpse from **ESMERELDA**, but she slaps him and he drops it.)*

ESMERELDA. How dare you! Indignity to a dead body! Stand not upon the order of your going, but go at once!

*(The **LANDLORD** dials his cellular telephone.)*

ESMERELDA. I'm old, but he's deaf.

LANDLORD. Yup, you can. Some old lady's trying to bury a goddamn dead cat in my back yard... The address is...

(**ESMERELDA** *grabs the cat and attempts to storm away, head held high. The* **LANDLORD** *exits after her; he's not quite finished with her.*)

LANDLORD. Hey!

ESMERELDA. *(off)* Hay is for horses.

LANDLORD. You're not putting that goddamn thing in my freezer...

(The **LANDLORD** *exits.)*

Scene Three
The Night Desk in a Police Station

(Officer **H.B. HACKETT** *[hereinafter* **H.B.***], trying to be civil, sits across a desk from* **ESMERELDA***, who is still holding the dead cat in the plastic bag.)*

H.B. Could you spell that for me, madam?

ESMERELDA. You mean, "would I"? M. E. R. L. I. N.

H.B. Your first name.

ESMERELDA. We both have the same surname, Quipp. Double P. My first name is E. S. M. E. R. E. L. D. A.

H.B. Was that E. L. B. A.?

ESMERELDA. Elba is where Napoleon vacationed. My name is closed with a D., as in Dostoyevsky, and A., as in Aristotle. Esmerel-da. Friends used to call me Essie.

H.B. Thank you, Mrs. Quipp.

ESMERELDA. Everyone presumes a woman is married past a certain age.

H.B. Miss Quipp. Sorry.

ESMERELDA. It's Mrs., actually. He ran off 40 years ago with an usher. Never saw him again.

H.B. Your husband ran away with an usher from your wedding?

ESMERELDA. A theatre usher. Slut.

H.B. Okay, Mrs. Quipp, then. Address?

*(***JENNIFER*** enters with a cardboard cup of tea and hands it to* **ESMERELDA***; she regards it with disgust.)*

ESMERELDA. Thank you, dear. Do you happen to have a china cup, even a tacky logo mug? Tea from cardboard tastes like… Cardboard tea. And a splash of milk would be lovely, please.

*(***JENNIFER***, amused, exits with the cardboard cup.)*

H.B. Right, I have your address here, as provided by your landlord.

ESMERELDA. What a frightfully nasty man. Utterly unsympathetic.

H.B. Was it your landlord who reported the incident?

ESMERELDA. Indeed, it was. I rest my case.

H.B. But he's right. It's against the local by-laws to bury dead pets in the back yard. What's your phone number?

ESMERELDA. Sorry, but I don't have a telephone.

H.B. Not even a cell?

ESMERELDA. Sorry, no.

H.B. How does your family reach you?

ESMERELDA. Through a medium.

H.B. Pardon?

ESMERELDA. I've spoken to them through a medium, you see. Someone who converses freely with those on the other side.

H.B. Of the Atlantic?

ESMERELDA. They're all dead.

H.B. Oh, ah, sorry. Then, how do your friends stay in touch?

ESMERELDA. They don't. The only one I had left was Merlin. I dreaded this day and it's happened, now, hasn't it?

(**ESMERELDA** *weeps a little, dabbing her eyes with a yellowing linen handkerchief.*)

H.B. When my dog died…

ESMERELDA. Oh dear. I'm terribly sorry; was he old?

H.B. Only ten, but he was a shepherd, and large dogs, they don't live so long.

ESMERELDA. It's those little yappy ones that live to be 15 or 20 to spite us. What was his name, your darling dear doggie?

H.B. *(softening)* Sarge. He was a great dog. Really smart. Used to steal Frisbees away from border collies.

(**JENNIFER** *returns with a proper china teacup and saucer, and a small carton of milk.*)

JENNIFER. Look what I found!

ESMERELDA. Well, aren't you just a darling. Thank you, dear.

JENNIFER. Sugar?

(**ESMERELDA** *shakes her head, sadly.*)

ESMERELDA. Diabetes.

H.B. Hey, me too.

ESMERELDA. I do miss biscuits and sweets.

H.B. Want a sugar-free cookie?

ESMERELDA. Oh, yes please! Lovely! Too kind, I'm sure.

(**H.B.** *digs through her desk drawer and hands a packet of biscuits to* **ESMERELDA,** *who carefully selects one.*)

H.B. Take a couple. Take the whole package.

(**ESMERELDA** *tucks the package in her carpetbag.* **JEN-NIFER** *exits.*)

ESMERELDA. Most kind. Thanks ever so.

H.B. Anyway, I took Sarge to his vet and they cremated him, and I got his ashes back in this sort of glittery little urn, and there was even a certificate of cremation. A sympathy card, too.

ESMERELDA. Yes, I did that with my other two cats, but I haven't the money to do that for Merlin.

H.B. Like the wizard?

ESMERELDA. Dear, dear Merlin. He was sleek and black with large orange eyes. Every Sunday morning – cats can count the days of the week, you see – he would come into the kitchen as I was preparing my tea and say, "Milk now, Mummy." Clear as a bell. Oh, Merlin...

(**ESMERELDA** *begins to really cry now, and she's embarrassed, wiping her tears away furiously.*)

ESMERELDA. I'm terribly sorry, Officer. He just died this afternoon. And he's my last... I should say, the last cat I'll ever have. And I can't even afford him a decent burial.

(**ESMERELDA** *places the cat's body on the desk and strokes it.*)

ESMERELDA. Dear, dear. He's very cold.

H.B. Because he's, um, dead?

ESMERELDA. The landlord refused to let me store him in the chest freezer, so I had to leave him in the shed until the nice constable came to collect us.

*(**H.B.** is tongue-tied; hesitantly, she reaches over and pats* **ESMERELDA** *on the hand.* **H.B.** *dials her phone.)*

H.B. Hey, Jennifer? Can you come here a sec? Bring a big green garbage bag, okay?

*(**H.B.** hangs up.)*

H.B. So, this charge your landlord wants to file, it's against you burying Merlin in his back yard because you can't afford to have him cremated or buried?

ESMERELDA. That's correct. I'm on a government pension and cannot make ends meet as it is, never mind incurring any unexpected expenses, I'm afraid.

H.B. Do you have anyone who can help?

ESMERELDA. I'm alone. My enduring soliloquy, so it appears.

H.B. Not one living friend?

ESMERELDA. Oh, a few of them are still alive, but they reside at a retirement lodge for elderly theatre people and are at the mercy of charity themselves, really.

*(**JENNIFER** enters with a large, green garbage bag.)*

H.B. This package here, it's Mrs. Quipp's cat.

JENNIFER. Oh!

ESMERELDA. My beloved Merlin; he's dead, unfortunately.

H.B. Since we're not sure if we're going to press charges...

ESMERELDA. Oh, thank you! Thank you, Officer Hackett!

H.B. ...Yet. We need the body put on ice for a bit. Until we decide... So, wrap it real well in the garbage bag, tie it tight, put a great big label on it saying it's not garbage, and stick in the freezer in the cafeteria. Thanks.

*(**JENNIFER** gingerly picks up the wrapped body, slightly grossed-out, places it in the garbage bag and exits.)*

ESMERELDA. The precinct secretary?

H.B. District social worker.

ESMERELDA. She's very sweet.

H.B. People person, not pet person.

ESMERELDA. Like we are.

H.B. Okay, look. I see that there's somewhat mitigating circumstances here, so I don't feel okay about laying a charge against someone... Someone like you.

ESMERELDA. You mean to say, an old person?

H.B. Do you think you could scrape together a small fine?

ESMERELDA. I have no food. My prescriptions consume most of my income. Avapro, Cortisone, Insulin, Lipitor. And that's just the first half of the alphabet.

H.B. That's a lot of drugs.

ESMERELDA. I'm a pharmaceutical lexicon! Something for you to look forward to in your advanced years.

H.B. If you could find some way to pay... I know a guy who makes a little extra cash picking up cans and bottles and selling them to the recycling companies.

ESMERELDA. Arthritis. Rheumatism. Gout. Sciatica.

H.B. Okay, so forget that idea.

ESMERELDA. My electricity is cut off; heat and hot water, too. I haven't a stick of wood for the fireplace. I've been stealing bits of crates from out back of the produce store just down the road a bit. I suppose that's illegal, too.

H.B. Taking somebody else's property is theft.

ESMERELDA. Even when it's merely junk?

H.B. Yup.

ESMERELDA. I figured I was doing the poor grocer gentleman a favour, relieving him of rubbish he would otherwise have to pay to have removed.

H.B. That's not how the law sees it.

(**JENNIFER** *enters with a coffee can and holds it out to* **H.B.**)

JENNIFER. Donations to fund the cat's cremation. I got the cafeteria lady to throw in twenty bucks; she wants the cat out of the freezer asap.

(**H.B.** *drops a five-dollar bill in the can.*)

ESMERELDA. How very kind.

JENNIFER. We're up to about thirty dollars so far.

H.B. We probably need a hundred, maybe more.

JENNIFER. I'm going to hit up the dispatcher next, then the hook… sex trade worker in the holding cell.

H.B. Is Penny still wearing off her latest hangover with us?

JENNIFER. Val's back. Penny's expected, as usual, later on.

H.B. Anyway, good plan. Those gals got more cash than the rest of us put together.

(**JENNIFER** *exits.*)

ESMERELDA. This is quite overwhelming. I'm deeply touched by all this generosity. Frankly, if Merlin had lived much longer, I'm not sure what I would have fed him.

H.B. How about a reduced fine? Maybe twenty bucks?

ESMERELDA. I'm three weeks behind on my rent.

H.B. Your landlord's adamant; he wants us to press charges.

ESMERELDA. And if I can't pay the fine?

H.B. You do the time. Overnight in the station slammer.

ESMERELDA. Oh dear, dear me; not terribly dignified for *une femme d'un certain âge*, is it, then…

H.B. Not with the company you'd be keeping. Hookers and petty thieves.

ESMERELDA. Completely unacceptable.

H.B. Drug addicts come in from the cold.

(**ESMERELDA** *likes something in those words of warning.*)

ESMERELDA. Is the cell heated?

H.B. I'll have to look up the minimum recommended sentence, but maybe a few days in prison, too.

ESMERELDA. Is there a library? A telly?

H.B. *(cluing in)* Yup, and there's hot water, too.

ESMERELDA. And a comfy chair? I brought my knitting.

H.B. I think we could find one, maybe in the chief's office…

ESMERELDA. Tempting!

H.B. And some mass of glop you might call breakfast in the morning, served with undercooked, greasy bacon.

ESMERELDA. Heavenly, but I must limit myself to one rasher.

H.B. And I could arrange for maybe a poached egg.

ESMERELDA. Delivered to my cell on a tray with flowers?

H.B. Sorry, no room service.

ESMERELDA. Could be a deal-breaker…

H.B. That's reserved for solitary.

ESMERELDA. Turn-down in the evening?

H.B. Self-serve.

ESMERELDA. A chocolate truffle and brandy?

H.B. That's a diabetes no-no.

ESMERELDA. Are the beds frightfully hard?

H.B. Never tried them myself.

ESMERELDA. I'm a tad lumpy. I prefer a softer mattress.

H.B. I heard they just retrofitted the cells; bought new mattresses.

ESMERELDA. Very tempting, indeed!

H.B. They're swamped with reservations…

ESMERELDA. I'll take it!

Scene Four
The Front Desk of the Police Station

(**ESMERELDA** *signs a document.* **H.B.** *signs also and hands one of two pages to* **ESMERELDA**.)

ESMERELDA. Thank you kindly.

H.B. Keep that in your files... Well, okay, your purse. Just in case you need to prove you paid for your, um, folly.

ESMERELDA. Though age from folly could not give me freedom, it does from childishness.

H.B. And please, Mrs. Quipp, if the landlord gets arrogant with you again, don't slap him. It's a miracle he didn't charge you with assault.

ESMERELDA. What's the sentence for that?

H.B. Have a nice day, Mrs. Quipp.

ESMERELDA. Thank you for your hospitality, Officer Hackett.

(**H.B.** *takes a phone call and makes notes as* **ESMERELDA** *goes to exit; she pauses and looks back at* **H.B.***; they exchange a friendly wave good-bye and* **ESMERELDA** *exits.*)

Scene Five
A Bank

(It's morning. Two **BANK TELLERS** *are open for business;* **BANK CUSTOMER #1** *and* **BANK CUSTOMER #2** *[hereinafter* **MILDRED***] are at the wickets.* **ESMERELDA** *enters, searches for the security cameras, waits until* **BANK CUSTOMER #1** *exits and a wicket comes free, and approaches the wicket where* **BANK TELLER #2** *works.)*

ESMERELDA. Good morning, Lucy!

BANK TELLER #2. I'm sorry; I don't think I recognize you.

ESMERELDA. Your name is on your tag. Don't you think that's a bit daft?

BANK TELLER #2. Daft?

ESMERELDA. For instance, a devious potential bank robber would know who you are.

BANK TELLER #2. It's just my first name. For security reasons.

ESMERELDA. Ah, but a charming bank robber could engage you in conversation as a means of distraction by using your name.

BANK TELLER #2. Do you have an account with us?

ESMERELDA. I don't need an account, do I?

BANK TELLER #2. In order to cash a cheque, you need to either have an account with us or the cheque needs to be drawn on an account that's with us.

ESMERELDA. No worries, Lucy, dear. I haven't a cheque to cash in any case. This is for you, Lucy.

*(***ESMERELDA** *hands* **BANK TELLER #2** *a note; she reads the note, looks at* **ESMERELDA** *and laughs slightly.)*

ESMERELDA. This is a most serious stick-up!

BANK TELLER #2. So I gather from your note. *(reads)* "Kindly place all of your bills, no coins if you please, in this bag, and it might be best if you do not scream. Yours truly, Esmerelda Quipp."

(ESMERELDA places a plastic grocery bag on the counter.)

ESMERELDA. Give me some money!

BANK TELLER #2. Any specific amount or just "some"?

ESMERELDA. Or I'll... I'll shoot!

(MILDRED hits the deck, screaming.)

ESMERELDA. Oh, shut up! I... I forgot my gun at home. *(to the BANK TELLERS)* Now... Oh, God! I forgot my line! Prompt!

BANK TELLER #1. This is a robbery?

ESMERELDA. Injurious time now with a robber's haste!

(The BANK TELLERS exchange confused, amused glances.)

ESMERELDA. "Troilus and Cressida."

(BANK TELLER #2 nods a message to BANK TELLER #1, who presses the police emergency call.)

BANK TELLER #1. Is that a Toyota?

MILDRED. Shakespeare.

ESMERELDA. "Crams his rich thievery up, he knows not how!"

(pauses) Oh, never mind.

BANK TELLER #2. Mrs. Quipp, right? Would you like this in large or small denominations?

ESMERELDA. A stack of unmarked bills, if you please.

(MILDRED gets to her feet.)

ESMERELDA. Sit! I mean, get down!

MILDRED. Are you all right? Esmerelda, is it? Don't I know you from somewhere?

ESMERELDA. I trod the boards at the Globe Shakespeare Festival for twenty seasons.

MILDRED. Mildred McGonigle; I was on the board of directors.

ESMERELDA. I remember you! You voted against better wages for actors! Oh, but if I had my gun right now!

BANK TELLER #2. Did you somehow slip out of the nursing home? And maybe get lost? Can we call them to come and get you?

ESMERELDA. Thank you for your kind offer. I am not any more lost than most people, and I do not reside in a home. In fact, it's getting so that I don't even think I have a home!

MILDRED. A little short on money?

(**MILDRED** *extends her hand with a wad of bills.*)

MILDRED. Here. I have extra. My husband won't even notice. I can give it to you or he can blow it all on his mistress. So, do me a favour and...

ESMERELDA. "We fail! But screw your courage to the sticking-place, and we'll not fail."

Give me the money.

(**MILDRED** *approaches* **ESMERELDA**.)

ESMERELDA. Not you! The teller! I want *only* the bank's money, and I want all of it, now!

BANK TELLER #1. *(to* **BANK TELLER #2***)* Did we screw her on a service charge, or something?

BANK TELLER #2. We screw everybody on service charges.

ESMERELDA. Move it! Oooh, that came off like Clint Eastwood!

BANK TELLER #2. Okay, Mrs. Quipp. You just stay calm, now. Take a deep breath. Count to ten backwards and...

ESMERELDA. I am not here for a surgical procedure!

(**BANK TELLER #1** *and* **BANK TELLER #2** *have a private confabulation.*)

ESMERELDA. Enough idle chit-chat. I mean, quit stalling! Load that bag with everything in your tills and make haste. Oh, do hurry up, please. The authorities will be here any minute!

(*The* **BANK TELLERS** *calmly begin emergency procedures,* **BANK TELLER #1** *dutifully dumping cash in the bag and then dropping below her wicket, and* **BANK TELLER #2** *cleaning a bit of money out of her till and putting the contents in the bag.)*

BANK TELLER #2. There's only a few hundred; will that get you by for now?

ESMERELDA. Just give me the bag and get down, if you please.

MILDRED. You can still have this. And I have a gift certificate for Starbucks. Take it.

ESMERELDA. I haven't lost all my pride, you know.

*(As **ESMERELDA** turns to leave, **BANK TELLER #2** ducks behind the counter, peeking over the top. **ESMERELDA** waves cheerfully at the closed-circuit camera.)*

ESMERELDA. Cheerio! Much obliged!

*(**MILDRED** shoves the gift certificate at **ESMERELDA**. **ESMERELDA** walks exceedingly slowly toward the door, and then pauses.)*

ESMERELDA. Just one more little thing, if you don't mind. Would you kindly ring me a taxicab? Happy Cabs have the nicer drivers, in my experience.

*(**ESMERELDA** resumes her slow exit. The sound of police sirens resonates from offstage.)*

ESMERELDA. About bloody time!

Scene Six
The Holding Cell in the Police Station Jail

(It is just before noon. In the cell are **VAL***, lounging on a cot,* **DOTTIE***, sitting on the edge of another cot, and* **GLADYS***, pacing.* **H.B.** *enters with* **ESMERELDA** *in handcuffs.)*

VAL. This club just got all geriatric.

GLADYS. The man lived; why am I in here? I'm being denied my legal rights as a citizen of this...

VAL. Put a cigar in it.

*(***H.B.*** opens the door and ushers* **ESMERELDA** *into the cell, undoing the handcuffs.)*

H.B. There you go, Ms. Quipp. Sorry to have to leave you in here with the real criminals, especially at...

ESMERELDA. At my age?

H.B. Ah, no madam...

VAL. She gets called madam and I am one. Go figure.

H.B. Your court-appointed lawyer, Mr. David, he'll be here in about an hour.

DOTTIE. He's a little hottie.

VAL. He's a nerd.

GLADYS. Why isn't my lawyer coming!

VAL. Because he's not my client.

GLADYS. Hooker humour?

VAL. If you don't laugh...

GLADYS. You cry?

VAL. You die.

GLADYS. You know, you look familiar to me...

VAL. Maybe I've done your husband.

DOTTIE. She tried to do him!

VAL. Looks like we both left the poor sucker alive...

GLADYS. Are you sure we haven't met?

VAL. Does he have my picture in his wallet?

*(***H.B.*** locks the cell door and turns to leave.)*

ESMERELDA. Incidentally, warmest congratulations on the new puppy.

H.B. Yeah, thanks.

ESMERELDA. Can't wait to see the snaps. Have you chosen a name yet?

H.B. *(sheepishly)* Captain.

ESMERELDA. Your dogs are moving up in the ranks! Well done!

VAL. You two know each other?

ESMERELDA. *(more formal)* Pardon me, Officer Hackett, would you be so kind as to tell me when lunch will be served?

*(**VAL.**, **DOTTIE** and **GLADYS** aren't sure if this newcomer is kidding or what; they snigger. **H.B.** stops, gathers her seriousness, and turns to **ESMERELDA**.)*

H.B. The roach coach is due any second now. Can I take your orders, ladies?

ESMERELDA. We get lunch from a coffee truck? What about the cafeteria?

GLADYS. I demand to see someone in charge!

H.B. This isn't prison, lady. It's a police station. Kinda like a halfway house for the pre-convicted.

GLADYS. I'm innocent until proven guilty! I want to speak to my lawyer! Get me a phone!

VAL. Get me lunch.

ESMERELDA. Yes, indeed; I'm finding myself a tad peckish.

H.B. Lunch comes from the roach coach, breakfast and dinner from the caf. Snacks are black market items.

ESMERELDA. Black market snacks?

H.B. The prisoners…

GLADYS. Excuse me!

H.B. The fine ladies of this cell – "jail birds" as I call them – have a network, about which I know squat, of suppliers that bring in stuff like chocolate and chips. I turn a blind eye. It's more complicated in prison, so I hear.

VAL. True, but there's more variety, including beer.

H.B. I did not hear that.

VAL. I like a Kir Royale at five o'clock.

DOTTIE. A who?

H.B. Does that answer your question, Mrs. Quipp?

ESMERELDA. I see; thank you kindly. It seems to me that the prison is… When will I be transferred to the prison?

H.B. You gotta stand up in front of a judge first.

ESMERELDA. When will the judge be available?

GLADYS. What if I'm here for days?

H.B. Look, Mrs. Bukovitch…

GLADYS. Symmington-Bukovitch…

ESMERELDA. Goodness! I was watching the telly in the electronics store just yesterday and saw your arrest!

GLADYS. Fame at last.

ESMERELDA. Sorry about your husband.

GLADYS. He lived.

ESMERELDA. Yes, sorry.

H.B. Look, I don't mean to be a pessimist, Gladys, but it's likely you'll be locked up for years. When attempted murder victims survive, they have this strange tendency to come down with a wicked case of verbal diarrhea.

GLADYS. His word against mine! He's a liar!

DOTTIE. What did he say?

VAL. Not much you can say when your neck's in a garrote.

GLADYS. I used a rif…

H.B. Hold it! Do not make me witness to a confession. I have a vacation planned and I'm not spending it the witness box.

ESMERELDA. A holiday! Lovely; where will you travel to? Personally, I used to adore a summer holiday at the beach in Brighton.

DOTTIE. Where?

VAL. I'm hungry. A girl's gotta keep up her strength.

H.B. Anyway, we pretty much wing lunch around here because we don't ever know how many guests we have dining with us midday, but you'll get breakfast and dinner made by our chef de cuisine, Madge Hodge, and brought in on nice little cardboard trays...

VAL. And flimsy plastic cutlery in case we were thinking they might be weapons of mass escape!

DOTTIE. Or murder! Why don't you just lie there and shut up.

VAL. You sound like a client.

ESMERELDA. Are there choices for breakfast and dinner?

VAL. For breakfast, you get to choose breakfast, and for dinner...

(The blast of the coffee truck's horn interrupts.)

H.B. I'm thinking four chicken salad sandwiches.

VAL. Hold the mouse turds.

H.B. And what would you jail birds like to drink with that?

VAL. A Stollie and tonic with lemon.

GLADYS. A diet ginger ale, but only Canada Dry.

DOTTIE. I bet the coffee's awful.

ESMERELDA. May I have a nice cup of tea, please?

H.B. Just a little milk, no sugar?

VAL. *(mockingly)* Please, Officer Honey Bunch?

ESMERELDA. Two per cent's fine if they don't have homo.

DOTTIE. They keep the homos in a different cell now.

H.B. Three bottles of water and a tea with milk.

*(**H.B.** exits.)*

DOTTIE. There used to be all this controspiracy...

GLADYS. You mean controversy?

DOTTIE. Yes, that, because the homo-sex-uals didn't want to be with the normal people.

ESMERELDA. The straight people, you mean. It's much more polite and respectful.

*(**VAL** gets up off the cot; she towers over **ESMERELDA**.)*

VAL. You some kind of fag-hag?

ESMERELDA. I'm a retired actress. In my many years on the stage I worked with dozens of gay gentlemen.

DOTTIE. Did ya ever have to kiss one?

ESMERELDA. Of course. When I played Juliet, my Romeo was gay.

DOTTIE. Put a guy in tights and that's what happens, eh?

ESMERELDA. Would anyone by chance have a cigarette?

GLADYS. You can't smoke in here!

(VAL tosses a pack of cigarettes to ESMERELDA, who takes one and sets it on her lips; VAL lights it for her.)

VAL. Got nothin' to lose, eh?

ESMERELDA. Indeed. Now, would you be so kind as to show me the proper way to inhale?

VAL. You mean, you're just starting now?

ESMERELDA. I've smoked on stage, of course. Fake cigarettes.

VAL. Why now?

ESMERELDA. Why not! As you duly noted, I've nothing to lose.

(As VAL demonstrates technique to ESMERELDA, H.B. enters with PENNY in handcuffs. PENNY is haggard, way past her best-before date, and drunk.)

PENNY. Thanks for the ride, H.B.

H.B. Val! Butt that out, now!

PENNY. H.B. is my D.D.

ESMERELDA. Oh, I'm not actually smoking, just learning. Sorry!

PENNY. Not that I actually have a car.

H.B. Now, please, Mrs. Quipp.

VAL. Not that there's any favouritism around here.

(H.B. escorts PENNY into the cell, undoes the handcuffs, and closes and locks the door. JENNIFER enters with the sandwiches and drinks, passing them through the bars.)

VAL. You stink like a distillery, Penny.

ESMERELDA. Goodness! It's still morning!

PENNY. I'll take that as a compliment from you, Val.

VAL. Mrs. Quipp, allow me to present Miss Penelope Farthing. Named for what she charges an hour.

PENNY. Sod off.

JENNIFER. Tea for Mrs. Quipp, just the way you like it.

PENNY. Morning's my cocktail hour. A minute past midnight to a minute before noon.

VAL. Hey, I ordered a water; there's only two.

PENNY. Who ya gotta screw around here to get service like that?

H.B. You missed lunch, Penny.

PENNY. Coffee. Just coffee.

H.B. Jenny, coffee for her high-ness, please.

PENNY. Double-double.

H.B. Black.

PENNY. Do they force you to get compassion training at cop college?

JENNIFER. Funny you should ask, because…

H.B. That was rhetorical, Jenny.

DOTTIE. Yeah, and dumb, too.

(*JENNIFER exits.*)

VAL. And this here's Dottie… And Gladys.

PENNY. Glad-ass? Another girl guide?

H.B. Where's the five-year-old, Penny?

PENNY. Um, I think I left her at Dolly's Daycare.

ESMERELDA. What a charming name!

H.B. That's a scam name for a drug den. Where is she, Penny? I can send a cruiser to go get her.

PENNY. That'd be great, Honey Bunch. If I could remember where I left her…

GLADYS. Is this about your daughter?

PENNY. I think I still have two of them.

ESMERELDA. I wish I had a daughter. Two would be lovely!

PENNY. Hey, grandma; where'd she come from anyway?

ESMERELDA. Esmerelda Quipp. Indeed, a pleasure to make your acquaintance, Miss Farthing.

PENNY. Farthingale.

DOTTIE. Is that some kind of bird?

PENNY. Jail bird. So, grandma, what's your deal? Snatch a purse from a little old lady?

VAL. The concierge at the front desk told us she tried to rob a bank.

PENNY. You? Ha! What's the freakin' world coming to?

H.B. Did you maybe leave her with your older daughter?

PENNY. Carmen?

VAL. I thought her name was Suzette.

PENNY. Hey, Vally, were you on the street last night? Was that you?

VAL. I had the night off.

PENNY. I hate it when the kinky guys wear armour.

VAL. Anyway, I steer clear of your turf.

PENNY. Damn straight. Best circuit in town.

VAL. Maybe when you retire…

PENNY. On what?

H.B. Penny, get your shit together. Where's your little girl? Where's Sunny?

PENNY. California? Never rains. Think I'll retire there. On the pimp pension plan. P.P.P. Speaking of which, I gotta skip to the loo.

H.B. In a minute.

VAL. Come on, Penny. Where did you leave your daughter?

PENNY. With her sister, yeah. Or was it my sister?

H.B. Unless you want child abandonment added to your rap sheet du jour, you'd best remember where she is. Fast.

PENNY. Okay, don't bug me. What day is this?

DOTTIE. Tuesday.

*(**PENNY** counts on her fingers.)*

PENNY. Okay, then she's in kindergarten all the live-long freakin' day and my sister pisses her up at 3:20 p.m. They'll dine on Kraft-freakin'-dinner and watch a movie with a cast of unreal characters. Jammies. Story. G'night.

ESMERELDA. I love reading stories to little girls. I act out all the parts, do different voices. What a lark!

PENNY. Hey, my back teeth are freakin' floating.

H.B. I think the potty's working. Plumber was in yesterday.

VAL. Now, *he* was a real hottie!

*(**PENNY** makes like she is going to use the toilet in the corner; **VAL** leaps up and draws the drape around it.)*

VAL. Sorry, Mrs. Quipp…

PENNY. *(yelling)* How freakin' middle-class does it get!

ESMERELDA. Thank you, Val. Terribly thoughtful of you.

H.B. I'll go phone your sister. I have her number memorized.

*(**H.B.** exits. **PENNY** draws back the drape and hollers after **H.B.**)*

PENNY. Tell her I said bye!

*(**PENNY** flushes the toilet, sways and stumbles. **VAL** helps **PENNY** get comfortable in the cot.)*

PENNY. You know, you're a gem, Val. I'm gonna mount ya in a freakin' gold setting and wear ya on my finger.

VAL. Mrs. Quipp, here, she used to be an actress.

GLADYS. *(to **VAL**)* That's it! Now I know where I recognize you from! You look like that actress, Rosanna something.

PENNY. No shit. You quit robbing banks for theatre?

ESMERELDA. The other way about, I'm afraid.

PENNY. Why?

ESMERELDA. Poverty; the great motivator, I suppose.

PENNY. No shit. So, you quit robbing theatres and hit banks?

ESMERELDA. Ah, not quite. You see...

GLADYS. Rosanna something...

PENNY. Not much money in theatre box officers... Boxers...Box offices, I'm thinkin'. Smart move.

VAL. Penny, Mrs. Quipp was an actress before she retired.

PENNY. From acting?

VAL. Yes.

GLADYS. It's like talking to a two year-old.

DOTTIE. Strung out on Froot Loops.

PENNY. So, Dottie, whatcha pilfer this time?

DOTTIE. I can't help it. It's a disease.

PENNY. So's addiction to vodka. What's your excuse, Mrsquipp?

ESMERELDA. For holding up a bank? I wish I could say I was practising for a role. I'm completely broke, I'm afraid.

PENNY. That's not Dottie's problem. Shoplifting's her hobby.

DOTTIE. My shrink says...

PENNY. Your shrink's probably one of my customers. I mean, who the frig ya think the shrinks bellyache to?

DOTTIE. He says I shoplift because my husband ignores me.

GLADYS. Look at yourself! No wonder!

DOTTIE. Yeah? And what about your husband, Gladys?

PENNY. Bump him!

ESMERELDA. Evidently she tried.

VAL. He didn't die according to the directions on the package. Better luck next time, Gladys.

PENNY. The woman from Glad!

ESMERELDA. That's actually quite humorous, given her hairstyle and all the various and sundry white apparel.

GLADYS. Next time use a gun, Esmerelda!

PENNY. So, you're the rich bitch from the newspapers? What a laugh! So, what? He can't get it up no more?

GLADYS. Do you mind!

PENNY. Or was the other well running dry?

GLADYS. You know nothing about me or my situation!

PENNY. I know your type. Too busy playing bridge, which means drinking freakin' gin gimlets, doing lunch, which means drinking chilled white, and buying freakin' Liz Claiborne cruisewear to satisfy your men. All your sex-starved husbands come see me. No droopy drawers with Penny!

(*JENNIFER enters with coffee, and hands it through the bars to* **VAL,** *who passes it to* **PENNY,** *who takes a sip.*)

PENNY. Horse pizzle!

ESMERELDA. I have a coupon for Starbucks, if you'd like.

PENNY. Great. I'll just check with Officer Honey Bunch, see if I can run down to the corner for a sec and grab a triple frappuccino. I'll come back, I promise...

ESMERELDA. I was just trying to be polite. No need to take out your frustrations on me.

PENNY. You're all pretty precious for inmate sisters. Oooh, my sensitive freakin' ears!

ESMERELDA. You're not a half-bad actress, Penny.

PENNY. It's a living.

(**ALFRED** *enters, briefcase in hand.*)

ALFRED. Penny, no part of you is sensitive.

PENNY. See what I mean? They've all had a little bite...

ALFRED. My wife is all I need.

PENNY. That's what they all say, right when they're cum...

VAL. Come on, Alfie. You're single.

PENNY. He is? You are?

ALFRED. I said it to bug Penny. It worked. Okay, E. Quipp?

PENNY. And ready! Let's go, Sugar!

ALFRED. Sorry... Emerald Equip?

ESMERELDA. Esmerelda Quipp? I am she.

PENNY. *(mimicking)* I am she.

ALFRED. Couldn't read my own writing.

GLADYS. Have you seen my lawyer?

ALFRED. What's his name?

PENNY. Dewey Cheatham and How.

VAL. That's original.

ALFRED. Now, Mrs. Quipp? We've got you charged with robbery… Robbery! Um, unarmed. Correct?

ESMERELDA. Yes, I mistakenly left my weapon at home.

ALFRED. Lucky you did. Armed robbery is a much more serious charge. Stiffer penalty.

ESMERELDA. Damn.

ALFRED. Let's see… Evidence…

ESMERELDA. Oh, I did it all right.

ALFRED. We'll plead this in the morning in front of a judge.

ESMERELDA. I just thought I could save you a little time, Mr. David. Guilty as charged, I'm afraid.

ALFRED. I have a report here written by the tellers, plus the recorded transcript and the surveillance camera footage. You did not carry a weapon, 100 per cent correct?

ESMERELDA. Correct. Yes.

(**ALFRED** *looks up from his notes and studies* **ESMERELDA**.)

ALFRED. Do you mind if I ask why you tried to rob a bank?

ESMERELDA. It was a promise I made to myself in the foolishness of my youth. If I live to be 80, I'm going to rob a bank and take up smoking. Well, I'm 80.

(**VAL, PENNY, GLADYS** *and* **DOTTIE** *burst out laughing.*)

ALFRED. Seriously?

ESMERELDA. I've still got it! Once an actress…

ALFRED. Mrs. Quipp…

ESMERELDA. Sorry. I needed to know if I could nail the character, just one last time. The truth of the matter is I am financially bereft and I desperately needed the money.

ALFRED. But when I viewed the tape, it all seemed... Well...

ESMERELDA. Perhaps civil?

ALFRED. Kind of a joke. The tellers didn't take you seriously. You were polite. Overboard polite.

ESMERELDA. Just because I'm destitute does not mean I have lost my good manners.

ALFRED. Look, it's almost dinnertime and I haven't had lunch. Humour me. What was going on in that bank?

ESMERELDA. I was robbing it.

ALFRED. With a courteous stick-up note? Come on.

ESMERELDA. When the police came, they found several hundred dollars on my person. That's proof enough, I should imagine.

ALFRED. Officer Hackett!

PENNY. Ooooh, now you're in big trouble!

ESMERELDA. So be it.

(**H.B.** *enters.*)

ALFRED. Torture chamber, please.

H.B. Right this way, sir. Will you be needing the rack? The chains are in place.

ESMERELDA. Ah, begging your pardon, Officer?

PENNY. Chill, grannie; that's what they call the private meeting room.

(**H.B.** *lets* **ESMERELDA** *out of the cell and locks up.*)

ESMERELDA. Shouldn't I be in handcuffs?

PENNY. Pretty much anybody could out-run you.

H.B. Ya know Penny, that mouth of yours...Try using it more productively.

PENNY. Send me your boyfriend, H.B.

Scene Seven
The Private Meeting Room

(**ALFRED** *and* **ESMERELDA** *walk downstage to two chairs; the cell upstage goes black.*)

ALFRED. Okay, Mrs. Quipp. Just you and me here. You, me and the unguarded truth.

ESMERELDA. Protected by the lawyer/client privilege?

ALFRED. Your secret's safe with me.

ESMERELDA. "Foul whisperings are abroad. Unnatural deeds do breed unnatural troubles; infected minds to their deaf pillows will discharge their secrets."
It's a simple matter of mathematics, Mr. David. I get set amount from the government in the form of a pension. It is not sufficient to cover my basic cost of living.

ALFRED. The pundits will say you gave up.

ESMERELDA. My career is over.

ALFRED. I guess because you're on a pension, you don't qualify for welfare?

ESMERELDA. I have left no stone unturned.

(**ALFRED** *responds instantly to his ringing cellular telephone.*)

ALFRED. Whatsup?… Tell him I'll be there within the hour. Bye.

ESMERELDA. Who was that?

(**ALFRED** *hangs up.*)

ALFRED. My secretary.

ESMERELDA. You were terribly short with her; ring her back and apologize. Go on… There's a good lad.

ALFRED. I'm a couple of hours behind here.

ESMERELDA. That's simply no excuse. I can wait. Ring her.

ALFRED. Look, Mrs. Quipp…

ESMERELDA. I'll speak not another word until you behave like the gentleman that your calling suggests. Go on.

(**ALFRED** *dials his cellular telephone.*)

ALFRED. Yeah, Wendy? Sorry 'bout that. I'm, um, stressed…

(**ESMERELDA** *nods her encouragement.*)

ALFRED. You didn't deserve that…

ESMERELDA. *(whispering)* Brusque treatment.

ALFRED. Brusk treatment.

ESMERELDA. Excellent good. And…

ALFRED. And… I owe you lunch… Okay, thanks.

(**ALFRED** *hangs up.*)

ESMERELDA. Is she a nice young lady, your secretary, Wendy?

ALFRED. I guess.

ESMERELDA. Lunch is an excellent good start and you can see how it goes from there.

(**ALFRED**'s *cellular telephone rings again.*)

ESMERELDA. Kindly do not answer that.

ALFRED. Excuse me?

ESMERELDA. It's frightfully rude. We are speaking about my situation. I require your undivided attention, if you please. I may be destitute now, but I did pay taxes in my day, and those have served, albeit indirectly, to deliver your wages.

ALFRED. Are you being treated for anything, oh, say, medical?

ESMERELDA. Diabetes. Arthritis. Glaucoma. Grief. Old age.

ALFRED. Dementia?

ESMERELDA. Out, alas! You'd be so lean that blasts of January would blow you through and through. – Now, my fairest friend, I would I had some flowers o' the spring that become your time of day; and yours and yours, that wear upon your virgin branches yet… Your maidenheads growing. – O Proserpina, for the flowers now, that, frighted, thou lett'st fall.

ALFRED. I studied Shakespeare at university.

ESMERELDA. Then identify the passage.

ALFRED. "Romeo and Juliet."

ESMERELDA. That's what they all say.

"From Dis's wagon! – daffodils, that come before the swallow dares, and take the winds of March with beauty; violets dim, but sweeter than the lids of Juno's eyes or Cytherea's breath; pale primroses..."

Can you cite that many lines from a play you don't know the name of?

ALFRED. "The Taming of the Shrew"?

ESMERELDA. "The Winter's Tale." Dementia? I think not.

ALFRED. Okay, I can probably get you off. There are three possible defences. Mitigating circumstances. That's one. Your age and general health. That might do it. Or, based on the video, and your waving to the camera, insanity.

ESMERELDA. You look tired. Would you like me to get Jennifer to make you a nice cup of tea? She's got the knack now that an old English lady has taught her properly.

ALFRED. Tea won't cure me, but thanks.

ESMERELDA. The trick is to warm the pot first and...

ALFRED. What's this about an illegal burial?

ESMERELDA. Ensure the water is at a rolling boil and...

ALFRED. I must have the wrong file folder.

ESMERELDA. Never use cheap teabags; a teaball is crucial.

ALFRED. If you babble on like that in front of a judge...

ESMERELDA. I am not insane. The one thing that is working quite well is my mind. Unfortunately.

ALFRED. Unfortunately?

ESMERELDA. Because it leaves me with an acuity that means I know the rest of me is coming unglued. I sometimes think dementia is bliss. One of my old co-stars is in a nursing home. Hasn't the foggiest what his name is – thinks he's Oberon – and gets lost going to the closet for his socks, if he remembers why he went to the closet in the first place, but he's full of fun and happily he keeps meeting new people.

ALFRED. How far behind on your payments are you?

ESMERELDA. My prescriptions are paid to current because the chemist does not extend credit. Everything else is far overdue.

ALFRED. When was the last time you ate?

ESMERELDA. I had a rather dry chicken salad sandwich at lunch. I could live off my body fat a day or two, but the trouble is, I don't have my pills or insulin with me. They took my handbag and all my medications are in it. And my knitting.

ALFRED. I'll take care of that right away. Are you depressed, Mrs. Quipp?

ESMERELDA. Don't be ridiculous! I'm English!

ALFRED. The system provides counselling…

ESMERELDA. I require a substantial influx of cash, not a psychiatrist!

ALFRED. You know, I wish I was independently wealthy.

ESMERELDA. That's very kind. Now, go home and get some rest.

ALFRED. I have work to do. You go up in front of the judge tomorrow morning.

ESMERELDA. Not to worry, then. I shall be pleading guilty and throwing myself upon the mercy of the court to give me a nice, long sentence. Officer Hackett tells me that the women's prison has recently been renovated. How charming!

ALFRED. Prisons aren't charming, Mrs. Quipp.

ESMERELDA. Everything is relative, Mr. David.
"Why have you suffer'd me to be imprison'd, kept in a dark house, visited by the priest, and made the most notorious geck and gull that e're invention played on? Tell me why."

ALFRED. Ah, sorry, but ah…

ESMERELDA. "The Two Gentlemen of Verona." The one madwoman of Shalott. It matters not. All relative. Dark corners find us, in a room or in our minds.

ALFRED. You know, if you said that in court, an insanity defence just might work!

(**ESMERELDA** *stage-shows dismay mixed with a touch of shock.*)

No insult intended, Mrs. Quipp. I need to get you off. You'll hate prison.

ESMERELDA. I've been in jail, but only for one stint.

ALFRED. *(leafing through the paperwork)* You have?

ESMERELDA. It was quite pleasant, really. The inmates showed great respect for their elder. They were simply fascinated by my stories of my days in the theatre, especially the occasion when the set collapsed when I was kissing my leading man and...

ALFRED. This is your second bank job?

ESMERELDA. No, no. I attempted to bury my deceased cat, Merlin, in my landlord's back yard and he called the police. I was fiscally unable pay the fine...

ALFRED. Right; that explains the illegal burial matter. So you served the time. What about the cat's corpse?

ESMERELDA. It's still in the freezer in the cafeteria.

ALFRED. This cafeteria? In the station?

ESMERELDA. Indeed. Next to the chips.

ALFRED. I had fries with dinner there last night...

ESMERELDA. Yes, French fries, as they call them here; why they do is simply beyond me.

ALFRED. And fish sticks...

ESMERELDA. However, more to the point, Jennifer is taking up a collection so that we can get Merlin cremated and I can have his ashes.

ALFRED. And frozen peas...

ESMERELDA. The ashes of my other two cats are in the same bag as my various and sundry life-saving medications... Perhaps I should just stop taking the lot of them.

ALFRED. Right, yes. We need to get you your meds... Stop them?

ESMERELDA. It seems a viable alternative, wouldn't you say? If I'm dead, the expenses will be somebody else's problem.

ALFRED. Are you, um, suicidal, Mrs. Quipp?

ESMERELDA. "Had she been light, like you, of such a merry, nimble, stirring spirit, she might ha' been a grandam ere she died; And so may you; for a light heart lives long."

Of course, we all die, Mr. David. Yet few of us have the luxury, if it can be called that, of choosing precisely when we'll take our final curtain call.

ALFRED. But are you considering...

ESMERELDA. I can't afford the cyanide, nor the length of sturdy rope, not even a prescription for too many sleeping pills.

There's nothing romantic in wrinkles

Or gravity making skin sag;

Old age is not for the feeble,

Suffocation is all in the bag.

I find I've become quite a nuisance,

A burden to state and to friends

Far beyond seeing the bright side;

Kindly tell me how this story ends.

I'm again wearing bibs and diapers,

There's spots on my liver and lung,

I never thought it would come to this,

So, top yourself when you're young.

ALFRED. Now, that's not Shakespeare.

ESMERELDA. Vintage Esmerelda Quipp.

ALFRED. I think you missed your calling. Maybe not... A rich poet? Oxymoron.

ESMERELDA. Oh, my hearing is dim,

My waistline's not slim,

My eyesight is weak

And it's not for the meek,

ESMERELDA. *(cont.)* This process of losing one's hold.
>   I'm stiff in the hips,
>   Too bold with my lips,
>   Subtlety gone with the wind;
>   My hair's grey and it's thinned.
>   Euphemisms are all left untold.
>   But the truth lies herein;
>   I take Scotch with my gin,
>   I've reverted to gruel,
>   Lack colloquial cool,
>   In this business of my growing old.
>   I take inventory,
>   A list rather gory,
>   And I know that my youth has been sold;
>   The devil may care,
>   But I've done my share,
>   And my house of cards I now fold.

ALFRED. Is there anything you haven't memorized?

ESMERELDA. My address.

ALFRED. I need to find a way to send you back home.

ESMERELDA. Home?

ALFRED. Don't worry. I'll find a way.

ESMERELDA. What's the prison term for murder?

ALFRED. Okay, then… I'll take you back to the cell and bring the meds… No, I'll bring the bag right in. Don't want to mess with the cat's ash…

(ALFRED *takes* ESMERELDA *by the elbow and helps her up; they walk upstage as the lights go up on the cell.*)

ESMERELDA. It's been quite some time since I had an escort!

ALFRED. It's been at least a week since I defended one!

(ESMERELDA *and* ALFRED *chuckle.*)

Scene Eight
The Holding Cell in the Police Station Jail

(H.B. enters with cots, pillows and blankets; she opens the cell door, lets ESMERELDA in, and places the items inside, locking it carefully. ALFRED exits.)

VAL. Heeeeeere's Honey!

H.B. Good evening, jail birds.

GLADYS. Rosanna Paderno!

PENNY. No monologue tonight?

VAL. Palermo.

ESMERELDA. The capital of Mallorca. I've seen her films; she's very good. For a film actress, that is.

VAL. Stage actors are better?

ESMERELDA. Different, perhaps more nuanced. Live performance affords no second takes.

H.B. So, guess what.

VAL. She really gets into her parts.

H.B. The ladies prison is shut down to new arrivals thanks to a mini-flu epidemic.

PENNY. You mean I have to share a room with them?

H.B. No, Penny; they have to share one with you.

GLADYS. But she reeks of booze. Is there another cell?

H.B. You can camp with the guys, if you want.

PENNY. The gentlemen's club. They just love dames who kill their hubbies. Yeah, yeah, innocent until found guilty.

(ALFRED enters with a carpetbag and a weary smile.)

ALFRED. Mrs. Quipp! Great news. Officer Hackett, open that door and spring Mrs. Quipp!

ESMERELDA. I beg your pardon?

ALFRED. Oh, you're welcome, Mrs. Quipp.

ESMERELDA. There are no words sufficient to express my gratitude.

(**H.B.** *unlocks the door and ushers* **ESMERELDA** *out of the holding cell.* **ALFRED** *hands her the carpetbag.*)

ALFRED. Officer Hackett, would you get a glass of water? Mrs. Quipp is late taking some of her meds...

ESMERELDA. Yes... *(picking up)* Yes! That's true... And when I'm late, they can have a terrible reaction, truly. Is there somewhere I could sit for a few hours... Just to be sure?

H.B. There's a waiting room. Maybe the staff lounge would be better. *(to* **ALFRED***)* How'd you swing this exactly?

ALFRED. Called the prosecutor at home, explained the circumstances; he waived the charges.

H.B. Just like that.

ALFRED. He was anxious to get back to CSI.

H.B. Just like that.

ALFRED. I'm done for the day. See you tomorrow.

*(***ALFRED*** exits.)*

H.B. I'm really sorry, Mrs. Quipp.

DOTTIE. Where ya gonna go?

ESMERELDA. To the waiting room, so it would seem. I can pretend I'm acting in "Waiting for Godot" and bide my time accordingly.

DOTTIE. God's in the waiting room?

ESMERELDA. Beckett.

DOTTIE. The Archbishop of Canterbury is waiting for God?

ESMERELDA. Samuel Beckett.

DOTTIE. Is that his brother?

ESMERELDA. No, and they both happen to be quite dead.

VAL. So much for God, eh?

ESMERELDA. Well, Penny's stuck in here for the night, so perhaps I'll have to take up her "circuit."

PENNY. Dolly's Daycare! Sure, it's kind of a joint for...

H.B. Drug dealers and addicts.

PENNY. Who just happen to be people, too.

ESMERELDA. Penny has a point, indeed.

PENNY. I even got a purpose.

VAL. They say we're all created equal, but we're not, are we.

PENNY. Tell them you know me. They'll find you a couch, someplace to sleep.

VAL. See ya, Mrs. Quipp. Parting is such sweet sorrow.

ESMERELDA. Thieves, prostitutes, murderers, even actors; we're all just people.

GLADYS. We'll be thinking about you, Esmerelda.

ESMERELDA. Like a dull actor now, I have forgot my part, and I am out, even to a full disgrace.

(Blackout.)

End of Act I

ACT II

Scene One
The Alleyway Behind a Restaurant

(Downstage or on the apron. It's night, and with ultimate stealth, as much as possible walking with a cane, **ESMERELDA** *enters and picks through a recycle bin, stuffing wine bottles in her carpetbag; she drops a bottle and it smashes.)*

ESMERELDA. Oh dear! Hark! Anon from stage left!

*(***ESMERELDA*** flattens herself against the wall in the shadows as a* **CHEF** *enters stage left and looks around; he sees the glass.)*

CHEF. Goddamn alley cats.

(The **CHEF** *dumps food in the trash bin, and two bottles in the blue box. He sweeps the glass into a dustpan and exits.* **ESMERELDA** *emerges, takes the bottles, finding a bit of wine in one of them; she studies the label.)*

ESMERELDA. My, my, what a marvellous find! Montrachet!

*(***ESMERELDA*** drinks from the bottle.)*

Diabetes be damned! So what if it kills me now!

*(***ESMERELDA*** holds the bottle, speaking to it.)*

I pray you, do not fall in love with me, for I am falser than vows made in wine.

*(***ESMERELDA*** lifts the lid to the trash bin and peers inside; she pushes back her sleeve and reaches in, then stops.)*

I'd rather go hungry.

(**ESMERELDA** *replaces the lid and counts the bottles in her bag.*)

ESMERELDA. Let's see then… The toy pistol is $2.99, plus tax, so I've got enough in recycle refunds, plus a dollar and thruppence left for groceries. Splendid! *(long pause)* What on earth am I talking about? Splendid?

(**ESMERELDA** *exits to the sound of a caterwaul.*)

Scene Two
Another Bank

(BANK TELLER #3 and MILDRED converse at a wicket. ESMERELDA enters with her carpetbag, and marches up to the wicket, pushing MILDRED to the side…)

MILDRED. Excuse me! Take a number!

ESMERELDA. This is a robbery! I am armed and dangerous! Stuff every cent from your bloody till into this bag and get on with it! I haven't got all day! Move it!

MILDRED. Esmerelda!

ESMERELDA. Do you have accounts at every flipping bank in town?

MILDRED. *(to BANK TELLER #3)* This is Mrs. Quipp. She was a fine actress in her day.

ESMERELDA. And now I'm an armed criminal. Rap sheet as long as Hamlet, full version.

BANK TELLER #3. Is this a joke?

ESMERELDA. No one takes me seriously. Observe: I have a gun, so do what I say or I'll blow this woman's brains out.

(MILDRED laughs. ESMERELDA draws her gun. Abrupt silence.)

ESMERELDA. You cast the tie-breaking vote to cap actors' fees and cut our pensions! *(to BANK TELLER #3)* Load this bag. Now! I have more than enough reason to kill this bitch!

(BANK TELLER #3 stuffs bills in the carpetbag while ESMERELDA holds the gun to MILDRED'S temple; she regards the gun.)

MILDRED. Made in China?

ESMERELDA. You consistently miss excellent opportunities to keep your bloody mouth shut!

(BANK TELLER #3 hands over the carpetbag to ESMERELDA, who backs out of the bank, and exits.)

ESMERELDA. *(off)* Taxi!

MILDRED. She pulled it off! Go, Esmerelda!

BANK TELLER #3. You know her.

MILDRED. Her? Serial bank robber. Good costume eh? You'd think she was maybe 80 years old!

(Sirens sound in the distance.)

BANK TELLER #3. I'm not sure that you're not an accomplice.

MILDRED. I wish I had her guts.

BANK TELLER #3. You have her name. That's what matters to us. And to the cops. You're not going anywhere…

Scene Three
The Holding Cell in the Police Station Jail

(VAL and PENNY play cards. H.B. escorts ESMERELDA in and opens the cell door.)

PENNY. Look what the Honey Bunch dragged in.

VAL. Esmerelda! We missed you!

ESMERELDA. I finished knitting those mittens for you, Val. I do hope you like them.

PENNY. Nothing worse than a hooker with cold hands.

ESMERELDA. Oh, Penny! I see you haven't lost your absurd sense of humour.

H.B. Here's your bag, Mrs. Quipp. Alfie will be in later. You know the rules.

PENNY. So, why here, Essie?

ESMERELDA. As opposed to?

PENNY. I dunno, like… Like… A convent.

VAL. Get thee to a nunnery!

ESMERELDA. I'm afraid I'm not Catholic.

VAL. I'm afraid I am.

PENNY. You're an actress, Essie, so just act Catholic.

VAL. Easy. Sin and apologize. Have lots of kids, but only if the Pope's their father. Stay in a bad marriage forever. And use guilt over sense every time. You'd look great in a habit!

ESMERELDA. At my ripeness, I am neither a virgin nor a novice. My only habit is thievery, evidently! I once tried to get myself a long-term room in a hospital, but they only had a bed in the psychiatric ward. Too noisy. Nasty smells.

H.B. That reminds me… Because this is your third visit, Jennifer will be here to fill in some forms; the powers that be need a psychological profile. Standard procedure.

ESMERELDA. I am but mad north-north-west; when the wind is southerly, I know a hawk from a handsaw.

PENNY. *(haughty)* Shakespeare, I presume!

VAL. "Hamlet."

ESMERELDA. How on earth did you...Oh. That's not quite what I meant. Permit me to apologize.

VAL. How does a hooker know Shakespeare?

ESMERELDA. I have criticized those who judged me and now I stand guilty of the same crime.

PENNY. Our crime was being born female.

VAL. Yeah, well, I wasn't born a hooker. In fact, it might come as a surprise to you, but I have a university degree.

PENNY. See, a B.A. doesn't mean bugger all, it means bugger anybody. For some of the gals, it means bugger anything.

ESMERELDA. I seem to have lived a rather sheltered life!

H.B. Roach coach coming in ten. Special today is tuna melt. Two bottled waters and a tea with milk. I'll find that cup.

   *(**H.B.** exits.)*

PENNY. Mystery fish with heated cheese facsimile on white bread. The whiter the bread, the sooner you're dead.

VAL. Since when do you care about nutrition?

PENNY. It's time I started taking better care of myself. I'm about to hit a special birthday, retirement age.

ESMERELDA. Oh, 65 isn't so old!

PENNY. I'm turning 45.

ESMERELDA. Oh dear.

VAL. That's the best-before date for us.

ESMERELDA. I do apologize...

PENNY. Racecar drivers, hockey players, firemen and hookers.

ESMERELDA. Frightfully sorry... Firemen?

PENNY. Burn-out.

   *(**VAL** groans; **ESMERELDA** laughs politely.)*

ESMERELDA. How are your girls? Sunny and Suzette?

PENNY. In training. Learning by example.

ESMERELDA. I'd love to meet them. I bet they're pretty.

PENNY. Yeah; I used to be. Their fathers? Who knows?

VAL. So, what got you thrown in here this time?

ESMERELDA. I successfully burgled another bank.

PENNY. So did the guys on Wall Street; they're not in here.

ESMERELDA. This time at gunpoint.

PENNY. Get out! Where did you get a gun?

ESMERELDA. At the dollar store. I went to the library and the nice librarian showed me how to use the internet on the computer, so I googled sections of the law and happily discovered that even a fake weapon – for that matter a concealed weapon that is merely alluded to – falls into the "armed" category, which results in a much stiffer sentence.

VAL. *(applauding)* Well done!

ESMERELDA. Did Gladys get out?

VAL. She's due back here today, on her way to prelim.

ESMERELDA. And Dottie... Did she get probation?

VAL. Out on bail, pending trial. Her old man's got bucks.

PENNY. So, how you gonna make the charges stick this time, grandma? I mean, we're onto ya.

ESMERELDA. I'm financially bereft, so I must resort to robbery.

VAL. Endless loop.

ESMERELDA. That's my story and...

"I am a kind of burr; I shall stick."

Val? Which play?

VAL. Hmm. Someone who won't let go. Romeo? Lady Mac...

ESMERELDA. No!!! Don't say it!

VAL. MacDonald!

PENNY. Ronald told me he wasn't married, but then they all do until...

VAL. Shylock? "Merchant of Venice"?

ESMERELDA. Very good, indeed! What's your degree? Literature?

(**JENNIFER** *enters.*)

VAL. Here comes Miss Masters in Social Work to save the downtrodden.

(**JENNIFER** *sits on a portable stool just outside the cell with a clipboard, forms and a pen.*)

JENNIFER. Mrs. Quipp, we need to do some paperwork, and unless you feel that the things I ask you are totally private, we can do it right here.

ESMERELDA. I have nothing to hide. I only wish that I did!

(**ESMERELDA** *sits on the other side of the bars from* **JENNIFER.**)

JENNIFER. Requesting silence from the peanut gallery, please. Okay, I've got all your basics here, and you say that you committed the two robberies to get money, right?

ESMERELDA. That's a common reason to rob a bank, yes.

JENNIFER. Any, oh, ulterior motives?

ESMERELDA. Such as?

JENNIFER. The underlying need to show off, in your case, return to acting? Maybe to regain a sense of importance? Grappling with control issues, resisting authority?

ESMERELDA. A rebellion against extortionate service charges, that sort of thing?

JENNIFER. Yes!

ESMERELDA. If that was my reason, I'd have done it years ago, now wouldn't I?

PENNY. Bank service charges are criminal…

JENNIFER. Penny…

ESMERELDA. It's time people realized that I am not off my rocker and that I simply needed money to pay my bills.

PENNY. I bounced a cheque last week and they charged me almost fifty bucks. That's a blowjob!

ESMERELDA. Why is that so hard – pun not intended – to accept?

PENNY. Ya think we do it for the fun of it? We got bills to pay, too.

JENNIFER. I just don't get it. You got charged and let off, so you went ahead and did it again.

ESMERELDA. Because I did not win a cent in any given lottery in the meantime. Ironically, I cannot afford to purchase a lottery ticket such that I might win said prize.

PENNY. Hey, Val, you ever won anything?

VAL. A lube job.

ESMERELDA. *(covering her ears)* Please, spare me the details!

VAL. *(loudly)* For my car.

PENNY. You have a car?

VAL. I won it when a new Quick-and-Slick Oil Change franchise opened in my neighbourhood. Or was it Dip Stick Quick?

PENNY. No wonder I never see you on the street. You've got a portable motel! Smooth!

JENNIFER. Okay, Mrs. Quipp, how did you afford to buy a gun?

ESMERELDA. I stole some select blue box items and sold them to a recycling dealer.

JENNIFER. Very clever.

ESMERELDA. Another crime. I am beyond reform! A threat to society.

PENNY. Rap sheets are us.

JENNIFER. So, you're trying to tell me you sold a bunch of bottles and cans and made enough money to buy a gun?

ESMERELDA. It was but a toy gun.

JENNIFER. Who told you that?

ESMERELDA. I paid under three dollars for it; it's plastic.

JENNIFER. They don't normally send plastic toy guns to ballistics for forensic examination.

ESMERELDA. You can't be serious!

VAL. Don't you watch T.V.?

PENNY. Duh. She had no electricity, Val.

JENNIFER. H.B. told me. It's gone to ballistics.

ESMERELDA. It sounds rather as though the police have gone ballistic. I assure you, it's a toy gun.

JENNIFER. Officer Hackett said it was loaded, too.

ESMERELDA. Nonsense.

VAL. Give it up, Essie. They've got your number. Major crime, you know; using a loaded gun to commit a burglary.

ESMERELDA. But…

PENNY. You hard-core armed robber! Lock her up! Throw away the keys!

ESMERELDA. Yes… Yes! That might be best. I'm incorrigible!

JENNIFER. It's my job to get to the underbelly of criminal activity. To figure out why you do this stuff and help you find your way to living crime-free, off the system.

PENNY. Praise the system!

ESMERELDA. The system is the problem. I cannot possibly live on that paltry sum. Val might remember this scene.

(**ESMERELDA** *stands and acts out a scene.*)

ESMERELDA. I am Romeo.

"The world is not thy friend nor the world's law: the world affords no law to make thee rich; then be not poor, but break it and take this.

I am now the apothecary.

My poverty, but not my will, consents."

VAL. I remember this! Now I'm Romeo.

"I pay thy poverty, and not thy will."

ESMERELDA. Now do you understand, Jennifer?

(**JENNIFER** *is silent, embarrassed.*)

PENNY. That sounds like something a pimp would say to his lawyer. I pay your poverty and not your will.

ESMERELDA. *(hamming it up)* Jennifer, my dear girl. I do appreciate your efforts at reforming my criminal mind and clearly devious character, but necessity dictates that if I am discharged, I will be added to that unsavoury list of repeat offenders and remain on it until I duly expire. Unless my circumstances are altered, which seems rather unlikely given my advanced age and unique situation, my problem stands, and my efforts to resolve it remain sadly unchanged. Don't see it as a failing on your part, dear. You are the epitome of kindness and caring. I have no doubt that you're excellent good at what you do. It's just that I am beyond rehabilitating. Old habits, you see, they in truth die hard. It's really no one's fault. I'm just too ancient to change my criminal ways. Sad but true. It may be more sensible to focus your noble efforts on the young and impressionable, those open to reform. I am hardened. Impenetrable. A lost cause.

(**ESMERELDA** *weeps.* **VAL** *and* **PENNY** *applaud.*)

PENNY. Can't teach an old actress new tricks.

ESMERELDA. What about an old whore?

(**PENNY** *and* **VAL** *crack up.* **ALFRED** *enters with* **H.B.**; *she unlocks the door, ushers* **ESMERELDA** *out, and locks it.*)

PENNY. Spoilsport.

H.B. Mrs. Quipp, your date with fate has arrived.

ESMERELDA. Oh, good afternoon, Mr. David. How nice to see you again.

ALFRED. Come with me, please, Mrs. Quipp.

PENNY. Torture chamber.

VAL. Old age. It's torture enough.

Scene Four
The Private Meeting Room

(Lights on the cell go black as **ESMERELDA** *and* **ALFRED** *walk downstage and take two seats.* **ALFRED** *reads his notes.)*

ESMERELDA. Jennifer is very sweet, don't you think?

ALFRED. Why, Mrs. Quipp? Why?

ESMERELDA. Because I think you're lonely.

ALFRED. The gun.

ESMERELDA. And there's something about Val, too. She's quite charming, despite…

ALFRED. You did it on purpose, didn't you?

ESMERELDA. Did you take lunch with your secretary yet?

ALFRED. This is not a social call!

ESMERELDA. Intention is nine-tenths of the law.

ALFRED. Frankly, I think it's a demonstration, a protest.

ESMERELDA. You could consider it that way, yes.

ALFRED. There are easier ways. You could get some Bristol board and a magic marker… March back and forth in front of the bank.

ESMERELDA. What good would that do?

ALFRED. It's a more sensible way to protest service charges.

ESMERELDA. I dare say it is, but I don't have a bank account. I use those payday loan dumps to cash my pension cheques. If this had been a protest, I'd have burgled them…

ALFRED. I know their fees are extortionate, but you're over-reacting, wouldn't you say?

ESMERELDA. I am known for realism, not over-acting.

ALFRED. I said…

ESMERELDA. In any case, I robbed them fair and square.

ALFRED. I got you off last time.

ESMERELDA. Your efforts were sadly commendable.

ALFRED. You're welcome.

ESMERELDA. Did I say "thank you"? I think not.

ALFRED. Now what? Do we run with the insanity defence? This is pretty insane, Mrs. Quipp.

ESMERELDA. I'll tell you what's insane! Forcing old people to choose between paying their rent or buying food and prescriptions. Penalizing us for a lifetime of tax-paying hard work with a gift of poverty that will see us to our graves. I have no idea how long I might live!

ALFRED. Yeah, well I have an idea where you might die.

ESMERELDA. In the ladies prison?

ALFRED. Armed robbery is pretty damn serious.

ESMERELDA. My dear Mr. David, if that gun had been real, I'd have gladly shot myself and got the whole thing over with.

ALFRED. That gun was real.

ESMERELDA. Don't be ridiculous. I paid two-ninety-nine for it at the cheap-goods shop.

ALFRED. That may well be…

ESMERELDA. I have the receipt!

ALFRED. Oh, it's a knock-off all right, made in China, but it's real.

ESMERELDA. I didn't purchase any bullets, though.

ALFRED. You probably bought it already loaded.

ESMERELDA. You mean I had the opportunity to murder Mildred McGonigle, and I blew it?
"And if you wrong us, shall we not revenge?"

ALFRED. As we speak, the police are investigating the store and its owners. Seems they're doing a bit of weapons trade on the black market.

ESMERELDA. Oh dear. But why would they sell a real gun to me for such a bargain price?

ALFRED. Maybe they thought you were a courier. I dunno.

ESMERELDA. Actually, that would be quite clever, wouldn't it? Having an old lady pull a stunt like that. I wonder if there's money in that sort of acting…

ALFRED. Maybe you stumbled in on a transaction in progress and they had to act normal.

ESMERELDA. "No sir," quoth he, "Call me not a fool till heaven hath sent me fortune."

ALFRED. So, the question is one of intent.

ESMERELDA. "As You Like It."

ALFRED. We're going to trial this time, Mrs. Quipp.

ESMERELDA. Excellent good!

"All purity, all trial all obeisance."

The Comedy of Errors.

(**ALFRED** *blows a gasket.*)

ALFRED. Mrs. Quipp! Do you even remotely get this? Either you do and you're crazy or you don't and you're insane! Shakespeare isn't gonna get you off. This is not a goddamn play! You seem to think prison is a hotel. It's hell. And for someone your age – yes, I am being politically incorrect – it will probably kill you. And I think you're a nice little old lady. I don't want you to die in some cold, grey institution.

ESMERELDA. A nice little old lady? Revolting.

ALFRED. Sorry?

ESMERELDA. Is that how you view me? Honestly?

(**ALFRED** *pauses to consider.*)

ALFRED. You remind me of...

ESMERELDA. Your mother.

ALFRED. My grandmother. Mea culpa.

ESMERELDA. Grey; it's a universal colour. You'll see.

ALFRED. Because she was smart, had a spark, a zest.

ESMERELDA. And was she destitute?

ALFRED. No. No, she wasn't. She had a, um, wealthy relative...

ESMERELDA. But she's dead.

ALFRED. Yes.

ESMERELDA. The great equalizer. Rich and poor are one.

ALFRED. You can avoid this stress, the whole nine yards by making an official statement about not being in your right mind, and we can plead...

ESMERELDA. Under no circumstances shall I plead insanity!

ALFRED. It's not what you think. Not like declaring you're completely crazy. More like you were out of sorts emotionally at the actual time you committed the crime. Crimes, plural.

ESMERELDA. Once when I broke my ankle – a tumble off the stage, most embarrassing, I assure you...

ALFRED. I don't know what else I can do to help you.

ESMERELDA. And when I had my shin and foot in a cast, people began to treat me differently, like I was utterly stupid. It made me wonder how physically handicapped people must feel.

ALFRED. I am so sick of being a public defender.

ESMERELDA. So, I would joke to everyone about having my I.Q. in a cast, but it wasn't funny. Not at all. It was pathetic.

ALFRED. I thought law would be a noble career.

ESMERELDA. And you want *me* to plead insanity?

ALFRED. Touché.

ESMERELDA. Perhaps I need a little more information. What happens with an insanity plea?

ALFRED. It depends. In this case, you'd probably get freed, likely with an assignment to a psychiatrist. If you really were a total certifiable nutcase, they'd likely send you to a penal hospital to live out the rest of your days. Sorry, I don't mean to suggest that...

ESMERELDA. My days are numbered?

ALFRED. Sorry.

ESMERELDA. You should be bloody well sorry; yours are numbered, too! Not even lawyers are immortal, although many behave as though they are.

ALFRED. "The first thing we do, let's kill all the lawyers."
   Henry the sixth.

ESMERELDA. Part two. You see? I am far from mad.

ALFRED. *(calling)* Officer Hackett?

   *(**ALFRED** guides **ESMERELDA** back to the cell, where the
   lights are up.)*

Scene Five
The Holding Cell in the Police Station Jail

(**H.B.** *enters and unlocks the door, waits until* **ES-MERELDA** *enters the cell, and then locks up; she exits.*)

ALFRED. We're talking each other in circles, Mrs. Quipp. I need to go away and consider your options.

ESMERELDA. Options? I am reduced to legal psycho-babble.

ALFRED. I can't just get you off the way I did before.

VAL. Shut up, Penny!

ESMERELDA. Excellent good! I wonder if they'll permit me to choose the paint colour for my cell. I am rather partial to English Tea Rose. Cheerful shade. Not overly pink. Compliments one's complexion. I do so loathe those sugary pinks. Frightfully tacky.

ALFRED. You know, maybe I should order a psychiatric assessment…

ESMERELDA. That and polyester sheers. Ghastly.

ALFRED. For myself.

ESMERELDA. Bats in your belfry?
"Ere the bat hath flown his cloister'd flight, ere, to black Hecate's summons."

VAL. The hamburger play.

PENNY. I thought it was MacDonald. Oh, right.

ESMERELDA. The shard-borne beetle with his drowsy hums hath rung night's yawning peel, there shall be done a deed of dreadful note.

ALFRED. That one I know… Mac…

ESMERELDA, VAL & PENNY. No!!! Don't say it!!!

ESMERELDA. When shall we three meet again in thunder, lightning or in rain?

VAL. When the hurlyburly's done, when the battle's lost and won.

PENNY. That will be ere the set of sun.

ESMERELDA. Brava, Penny!

ALFRED. Never mind, I'll just walk right into an asylum and tell them I'm a lawyer.

ESMERELDA, VAL & PENNY. Fair is foul, and foul is fair, hover through the fog and filthy air.

ESMERELDA. I could start a theatre troupe! Bards Behind Bars.

VAL. Actors Within Borders.

PENNY. No Exit.

ESMERELDA. I had no idea you read Sartre!

PENNY. Who started to read?

ALFRED. You'll be lucky to get a couple of hours watching soap operas on T.V. Prison is not where you want to be, Mrs. Quipp, trust me.

ESMERELDA. A pleasant little halfway house, perhaps?

ALFRED. Just you and nine other parolees?

ESMERELDA. Is there one in Stratford?

ALFRED. Doubtful; there's a long waiting list at all of them.

ESMERELDA. Well, I can't go back to my old flat.

ALFRED. I assume you've been evicted, anyway.

ESMERELDA. There was nothing to evict. Perhaps an old pair of shoes I left in the closet; everything else is in my carpetbag, even the ashes of Guinevere and Arthur.

ALFRED. So, what's next? A bank robber and two hookers do Camelot?

ESMERELDA, VAL & PENNY. *(singing)*

WHERE ONCE IT NEVER RAINED 'TIL AFTER SUN-DOWN.

ESMERELDA. Now it rains all bloody day and night and there's no castle to shelter me. My armour has rusted.

ALFRED. I'm going to consult with a colleague. Try to figure out something. In the meantime, try to refrain from any more criminal stuff. You're exhausting me.

ESMERELDA. As long as I am in here, society is safe.

*(**ALFRED** exits.)*

ESMERELDA. I need a cigarette.

PENNY. Ditto.

(*VAL hands cigarettes to* **ESMERELDA** *and* **PENNY**; *all three light up.* **ESMERELDA** *coughs.*)

ESMERELDA. Kill me to-morrow; let me live to-night!

(*VAL hands another cigarette to* **ESMERELDA**.)

VAL. Here, have another one…

(*VAL pops a cigarette in* **ESMERELDA**'s *mouth.*)

ESMERELDA. Truly, Val, Gladys was correct; you do resemble Rosanna Palermo. I watched one of her films a few weeks ago in the appliance department at Sears.

PENNY. What we could do if we had that kind of money! She's gotta be richer than Glad-ass.

VAL. What would you do with a million bucks, Penny?

PENNY. Freedom 45. Pay all my fines, get out of here and retire. Raise my girls like a real mother. How middle-class is that, eh? Some dream.

ESMERELDA. It's a perfect dream, Penny.

VAL. I guess we know what you'd do Esmerelda…

ESMERELDA. Certainly I'd keep what I needed to live… Of course, I don't know how long that might be. I'd give the rest to charity, to the lodge for retired actors and a cat sanctuary.

PENNY. A cat-house… Like Dolly's Daycare?

ESMERELDA. That, too. Yes! Capital idea! They were very kind to me that night. Thank you for referring me. Nice place to visit, but I wouldn't wish to live there.

PENNY. An old whore named Dolly Duke won the lottery and retired; when she died, she left the house to her old friends from the street.

VAL. Quipp's Quarters.

ESMERELDA. Val's Vagrant Villa.

PENNY. Penny's only home.

Scene Six
The Night Desk in the Police Station

(H.B. sits at her desk, typing. ALFRED enters and sits across from H.B.; she stops typing and waits.)

ALFRED. What do you make of her?

H.B. Are you kidding me?

ALFRED. Do you think she's demented?

H.B. You're yanking my chain, right?

ALFRED. I guess she must have been telling the truth; she needed the money.

H.B. She's a sly old fox and she's out-foxed you.

ALFRED. Even if I get her off, she's still destitute. Problem not solved. And if she robs another bank… You know, one day some armed guard is going to blow her brains out.

H.B. Despite her money problems, she's amazingly upbeat. Jennifer agrees; she's not depressed.

ALFRED. Or insane. Just slightly…eccentric.

H.B. If we could take away her need to pay rent, she'd be okay. She can afford food and her meds. Either or. You have a spare room at your house. Didn't your grandmother live there?

ALFRED. I've turned it into a home office. What about your sun porch?

H.B. Not heated in winter. She'd never get up the front steps, either.

(JENNIFER enters.)

ALFRED. Well, we can't let her die on the streets.

JENNIFER. What's happened to Penny this time?

H.B. Mrs. Quipp.

JENNIFER. I collected enough to get Merlin cremated!

H.B. I'll take him to the vet right now and get that done.

ALFRED. Then I can eat fish and chips again.

(H.B. exits.)

ALFRED. I'm sorry about last night.

JENNIFER. I'd give you another chance if you asked.

ALFRED. I got buried in my work…

JENNIFER. That's pretty lame, Alfie.

ALFRED. Okay, so I completely caved. Sorry.

JENNIFER. Let's just start over.

ALFRED. I get a second chance?

JENNIFER. Not everybody does.

ALFRED. Well… For our first date, how'd you like you to come over to my place, have some pizza, maybe a beer…

JENNIFER. Beer is not romantic…

ALFRED. Wine and you can help me figure out what to do about Mrs. Quipp; we're in court at ten in the morning.

JENNIFER. Now, that's romantic!

ALFRED. Really?

JENNIFER. It is to me. I care about her, too.

ALFRED. There's got to be a solution. Got any ideas?

JENNIFER. I'm a social worker, Alfred; I undo bad ideas, but have none of my own.

Scene Seven
A Courtroom

(**JUDGE JULIUS** *sits at the bench reading a set of notes;
she continues to read the pages throughout this scene,
intermittent with her lines.* **ESMERELDA** *and* **ALFRED**
stand before **JUDGE JULIUS**. *Present are* **JENNIFER, H.B.**
and **MILDRED**.)

JUDGE JULIUS. This is insane!

(**JUDGE JULIUS** *throws some of the papers at* **ALFRED**.)

ALFRED. Can't say I didn't warn you, Your Honour.

JUDGE JULIUS. Mr. David, you can't punctuate your way
out of an affidavit, and your grammar should get life
with no parole. How the hell'd you get a law degree?
Mrs. Quipp, if I were you I'd demand a lawyer who can
spell. Woman, speak up!

ESMERELDA. I regret to say, Your Honour, that my courtroom experience is limited to act four, scene one of
"The Merchant of Venice."

"Ready, so please your grace."

JUDGE JULIUS. *(glancing up)* Works for me.

ESMERELDA. I played Portia. She played a doctor of laws.

"Of a strange nature is the suit you follow: yet in such
rule, that the Venetian law cannot impugn you as you
do proceed – you stand within his danger, do you not?"

ALFRED. Mrs. Quipp, I warned you...

JUDGE JULIUS. With all due respect or lack thereof, shut
up, Mr. David. I don't get to the theatre much any
more because of you hot-shot young lawyers wasting
my time with crappy punctuation. Despite that, I am
beginning to see a pattern emerging from this literary
catastrophe of yours.

How does it go, again, Mrs. Quipp?

"And thus a while the fit will work on him; anon, as
patient as the female dove, when her golden couples
are...?"

ESMERELDA. When *that* her golden *couplets* are *disclos'd…*

JUDGE JULIUS. His silence will sit drooping.

(**JUDGE JULIUS** *pauses, staring down* **ALFRED**.)

JUDGE JULIUS. *(louder)* His silence will sit drooping!

(**ALFRED** *sits.* **JUDGE JULIUS** *resumes reading, tossing the odd page as she goes.*)

ESMERELDA. Shouldn't I be entering a plea?

JUDGE JULIUS. I'll be the judge of that… Go on.

ESMERELDA. Very well, then, Your Honour.
"The quality of mercy is not strain'd; It droppeth as the gentle rain from heaven upon the place beneath: it is twice bless'd…"

JUDGE JULIUS. And banks you twiceth robbed, according to this glittering document. How old are you, Mrs. Quipp?

ESMERELDA. Eighty.
I never knew so young a body with so old a head.

JUDGE JULIUS. Then you know better.

ESMERELDA. Quite so, Your Honour. Flagrant disregard for the law. Shameful, indeed.

JUDGE JULIUS. But I bet you can spell.

ESMERELDA. On top of that I attempted to bury my dead cat in my landlord's yard.

JUDGE JULIUS. Now there's grounds for a public hanging!

ESMERELDA. And I stole wooden crates from a green grocer and wine bottles from a restaurant recycle bin.

JUDGE JULIUS. Roll in the gallows and summon Charles Dickens to the stand!

ESMERELDA. I have a terribly long rap sheet, Your Honour. I was arrested once in Trafalgar Square for shouting, "Democracy is a Sham! The Prime Minister is an Elected Dictator!"

JUDGE JULIUS. That I can't convict you for; you're right.

ESMERELDA. And I once stole a scene from the lead actress.

JUDGE JULIUS. Blindfold the prisoner and prepare the firing squad!

ESMERELDA. It was Jessica Tandy.

JUDGE JULIUS. Never mind! I'll shoot her myself!

ESMERELDA. I pinched a pencil from my father when I was six; that started the whole mess rolling. My life of crime.

(**ESMERELDA** *hangs her head, with great dramatic flare.*)

JUDGE JULIUS. There's no law says you have to plead guilty; we can go to trial.

ESMERELDA. It would take forever, which in my case could be too long a stretch. Besides, I did it. I'm guilty. I confess.

"He was not born to shame; upon his brow shame is ashamed to sit."

ALFRED. *(standing)* I beg your pardon, Your Honour, there is some question as to Mrs. Quipp's mental agility. I've ordered a full psychiatric assessment.

ESMERELDA. To which I refuse to submit! Agility, my fanny!

"He would drown the stage with tears, and cleave the general ear with horrid speech, make mad the guilty, and appall the free, confound the ignorant, and amaze, indeed, the very faculty of eyes and ears."

I am not mad. Not even a titch of senility. I know precisely where I left my car keys and I haven't had a car since 1965.

JUDGE JULIUS. But where did you leave the car?

ESMERELDA. Ah ha! A trick question!

"I know a trick worth two of that."

ALFRED. Mrs. Quipp, please!

ESMERELDA. Henry four, part one.

JUDGE JULIUS. What's this "no fixed address" business?

ESMERELDA. I've been evicted, Your Honour.

JUDGE JULIUS. It says here that you helped the police bust an illegal firearms racket.

ESMERELDA. I did?

JUDGE JULIUS. Ten arrests in three countries, sixty million bucks worth of contraband guns, rifles and ammo, a couple of million in cocaine, and a stolen Ferrari F-50.

ESMERELDA. Of course! The dollar store!

JUDGE JULIUS. Good work, Mrs. Quipp.

ESMERELDA. Goodness gracious me, Your Honour!

JUDGE JULIUS. Now, as I understand it, the reward for this could be half a million bucks, maybe more.

ESMERELDA. Good lord!

JUDGE JULIUS. But there's this little matter of you being arrested for armed robbery... You'd be unable to collect your reward from a jail cell. Not quite legit.

ESMERELDA. Oh dear.

JUDGE JULIUS. And there are all those other extremely, very, very serious charges. I see you did the time, though. Hmmm.

ESMERELDA. Merlin was cremated yesterday.

JUDGE JULIUS. You can't collect that reward if you're in the slammer. What did you say?

ESMERELDA. Merlin was finally cremated yesterday. I have Arthur and Guinevere right here in my carpetbag.

JUDGE JULIUS. Is that so?

ESMERELDA. Though justice be thy plea consider this – that in the course of justice none of us should see salvation: we do pray for mercy.

JUDGE JULIUS. This woman's crazy! She thinks she's cremated half of Camelot! What did you do with Lancelot?

ESMERELDA. My former husband took him when he ran off with the usher. They live in the Cotswalds. Lovely spot. I must assume that Lancelot has passed on by now, or he would be at least thirty. Ancient by any standards.

JUDGE JULIUS. So, Mrs. Quipp. Had any spells lately? Feeling, oh, I don't know, slightly...insane?

ESMERELDA. Mr. David!

(**ALFRED** *stands next to* **ESMERELDA**, *nudges her slightly.*)

ESMERELDA. Spells... Marginal insanity... Prompt!

ALFRED. She displays behaviour consistent with senility, Your Honour. I would like to call a witness.

JUDGE JULIUS. I would like to call a mistrial! Proceed.

ALFRED. Calling Mildred McGonigle to the stand.

(**MILDRED** *takes the stand and picks up the Bible.*)

JUDGE JULIUS. Do you swear to tell the truth, the whole truth and nothing but the truth, so help you dog? God. So help you God?

MILDRED. I do.

ALFRED. Mrs. McGonigle, you are the only witness to both of the bank robberies executed by the defendant, Mrs. Esmerelda Quipp.

ESMERELDA. With two Ps.

MILDRED. I was personally robbed of a Starbucks gift certificate.

JUDGE JULIUS. Don't they just give those away?

ESMERELDA. Double P... Here, puss-puss...

ALFRED. You are also a former member of the board of directors at the Globe Shakespeare Festival; is that correct?

MILDRED. Yes.

ESMERELDA. Show me the steep and thorny way to heaven...

ALFRED. So, you had the opportunity to observe Mrs. Quipp in her right mind.

MILDRED. Oh, yes. Well, except when she played Ophelia. Perfect madness! Excellent work, by the way, Esmerelda.

ESMERELDA. Oh, heavenly powers, restore him!

ALFRED. In the course of the bank heists, did you observe any words or actions made by the defendant that would suggest she was in a state outside of her normal self?

MILDRED. I certainly did!

ALFRED. Would you please elaborate on your observations, Mrs. McGonigle. How did Mrs. Quipp behave that suggested to you she was in a momentary state of insanity?

MILDRED. Well, she was really polite the first time.

JUDGE JULIUS. Good manners are insane? I admit, they're rare these days, but hardly crazy.

MILDRED. But she's an actor. They're all rude. Try getting an autograph.

JUDGE JULIUS. Point taken.

MILDRED. The second time…

JUDGE JULIUS. Do you have accounts at every flipping bank in town?

MILDRED. It was like she was possessed, swearing, talking to herself, and she pulled a gun; pointed it right at my temple.

ESMERELDA. It was, I thought, a toy pistol, Your Honour…

JUDGE JULIUS. You are nuts, Mrs. Quipp! Trying to rob a bank with a toy pistol!

MILDRED. There was an evil look in her eye; she meant business. This was definitely not acting.

ESMERELDA. How many ages hence shall this our lofty scene be acted o'er, in states unborn, and accents yet unknown!

Cassius. "Julius Caesar."

MILDRED. In the first robbery, she was acting out "Troilus and Cressida." How crazy is that? I mean, who actually goes to see that one?

JUDGE JULIUS. Insane!

MILDRED. And after the teller dumped her till in the bag, she went out and hailed a cab!

JUDGE JULIUS. A cab! Cabs are for wealthy people. Do you have a problem with the bus, Mrs. Quipp?

ESMERELDA. I was blowing a bit of my spoils, Your Honour.

ALFRED. Thank you, Mrs. McGonigle; you may step down.

ESMERELDA. Rhubarb, rhubarb, rhubarb…

(**MILDRED** *leaves the stand.*)

ALFRED. Calling Police Officer Honey Bunch Hackett to the stand.

ESMERELDA. That's your real name?

(**H.B.** *takes the stand and raises her right hand.*)

JUDGE JULIUS. Do you swear to tell the truth, the whole truth and nothing but the truth, so help you God?

H.B. So help me, dog.

ESMERELDA. And how is Captain? I bet he's grown!

ALFRED. In your time presiding over the holding cell, did you observe any strange behaviour exhibited by the defendant?

ESMERELDA. I had rather be a dog, and bay the moon, than such a Roman.

H.B. By the time she arrived in custody, she'd pretty much calmed down.

ALFRED. So, would you conclude that her times of madness were episodic?

H.B. Yes. Mrs. Quipp is a remarkably intelligent woman, save for the odd moment of complete craziness, like knitting.

ESMERELDA. The spinsters and the knitters in the sun and the free maids that weave their thread with bones…

JUDGE JULIUS. "Twelfth Night."

ESMERELDA. …Do us to chant it; it is silly sooth, and dallies with the innocence of love…

JUDGE JULIUS & ESMERELDA. Like the old age.

ALFRED. What did she do in your presence that would indicate she has her moments?

H.B. She insisted on having her tea in a china cup.

ESMERELDA. With a splash of milk.

JUDGE JULIUS. Where did she think she was? The Ritz?

ALFRED. Any other evidence of insanity?

H.B. Well, I mean… She's an actor; how crazy is that!

JUDGE JULIUS. Second only to a career in law.

ESMERELDA. Because he is an actor, I shall not degrade his profession!

JUDGE JULIUS. What play is that from?

ESMERELDA. Not old Wills this time; Samuel Johnson speaking about his friend, the actor David Garrick, who, for the record, is buried in Westminster Abbey. How many lawyers do you suppose are interred there?

H.B. And she took up smoking.

(All, except **ESMERELDA**, *utter a stage gasp.)*

JUDGE JULIUS. Shocking! Now, that's certifiable!

ALFRED. Anything more?

ESMERELDA. Make the Moor thank me, love me, and reward me for making him egregiously an ass…

ALFRED. Um, Mrs. Quipp…

ESMERELDA. And practising upon his peace and quiet, even to madness!

H.B. I stand proven.

ALFRED. Thank you, Officer Hackett.

*(***H.B.*** steps down and takes her seat.)*

JUDGE JULIUS. Well, Mrs. Quipp, what say you now?

ESMERELDA. Hector is dead; there is no more to say.

JUDGE JULIUS. Did you cremate him, too?

ESMERELDA. Actually, it was Ector, not Hector, I cremated. Sir Ector de Maris, the son of King Ban of Berwick.

JUDGE JULIUS. Camelot?

ESMERELDA. A Knight of the Round Table, yes, Your Honour. All of my cats have been thus knighted. Except Merlin, of course.

JUDGE JULIUS. That makes it perfectly clear for me. Thank you, Mrs. Quipp. Please, take a seat.

*(***ESMERELDA*** sits.)*

JUDGE JULIUS. Evidently, Mrs. Esmerelda Quipp, with two Ps, is an authority on Shakespeare, but like her pal Hamlet, she has experienced occasional bouts of hysteria, primarily when she does her banking. According to the psychological assessment made by Jennifer Doer, social worker, there is an actual condition, albeit obscure, that describes a morbid fear of financial institutions: Exchequeraphobia. This condition is exacerbated by lack of funds. The fear of the fear of not having money begets greater fear. Understand?

ESMERELDA. Yes, oddly enough, I do believe I do, Your Honour.

JUDGE JULIUS. Then, you're in a normal state now.

ESMERELDA. It's all relative.

JUDGE JULIUS. Therefore, given what I have read and heard this morning, I am compelled to render my judgment that Esmerelda Quipp was insane at the time she committed the two bank robberies, and grieving insanely when she attempted to bury her cat. As far as stealing scenes, that's Jessica Tandy's problem.

ESMERELDA. She's dead, Your Honour.

JUDGE JULIUS. Just tell me you didn't try to bury her in somebody's yard.

ESMERELDA. I haven't a shovel to my name.

JUDGE JULIUS. On to the sentencing. I hereby sentence you, Esmerelda Quipp, to six weeks of Nicorette, and weekly therapy for the rest of your days.

ESMERELDA. I really don't need a psychiatrist, Your Honour...

JUDGE JULIUS. Massage therapy. Helps with arthritis. Officer Hackett, I believe you can now arrange for Mrs. Quipp's reward money to be released. Mrs. Quipp, you're free to go.

ESMERELDA. It's been a pleasure, Your Honour. Have a lovely afternoon. Thank you very kindly.

JUDGE JULIUS. Adjourned.

ESMERELDA. "He fumbles up into a loose adieu."

MILDRED. "Troilus and Cressida." I'll never view it the same way again.

(**ESMERELDA** *is helped by* **JENNIFER**, *and they exit.* **MILDRED** *and* **H.B.** *exit behind them.* **JUDGE JULIUS** *approaches* **ALFRED**.)

JUDGE JULIUS. Well done, Mr. David. An act of true kindness.

ALFRED. An Oscar-worthy performance on your part, Judge!

JUDGE JULIUS. That could have been me ten, twenty years from now. If I hadn't married into money, got put through law school, and become a judge, I'd be in her position. I was lucky. That's all. Just lucky. What worries me is that there are thousands of Esmerelda Quipps out there and I can't do the same for all of them.

ALFRED. The war may rage on, but at least this battle is won.

JUDGE JULIUS. The next time my grandson points his water pistol at me...

ALFRED. You'll go ballistic?

(**JENNIFER** *enters and* **JUDGE JULIUS** *exits.*)

ALFRED. Well, your idea worked, Jennifer.

JENNIFER. My first idea ever! I wonder what my second idea will be? Oh!

(**JENNIFER** *kisses* **ALFRED**, *much to his surprise and pleasure.*)

ALFRED. Now I'm looking forward to your third idea!

JENNIFER. Me too!

(**ALFRED** *holds out his arm for* **JENNIFER**; *she takes it.*)

ALFRED. Mrs. Quipp would approve.

JENNIFER. What do you think of an Adopt-a-Grannie business?

(**ALFRED** *and* **JENNIFER** *exit, arm in arm.*)

Scene Eight
The Holding Cell in the Police Station Jail

(PENNY and VAL lounge in the cell as ESMERELDA enters, dressed in a new coat and hat.)

VAL. Esmerelda! Wow, look at you!

PENNY. What'd you rob this time, grandma? A ladies clothing store?

ESMERELDA. Indeed; one for old biddies. Fashions for the femme *fatal.*

VAL. All dressed up with nowhere to go?

ESMERELDA. I have a few errands to run, actually. I have to see Mr. David to sign the papers for the house I bought, then pop round to the S.P.C.A. to choose a cat. This one will be Galahad, methinks. Dinner at eight with Judge Julius and her husband. No rest for the vindicated!

PENNY. You bought a house?

ESMERELDA. I bought Dolly's Daycare, and I'm having it renovated.

PENNY. You did rob another bank!

ESMERELDA. It will provide free accommodations for women who are broke… Actresses, hookers… Any woman who finds herself in need of shelter and food, company and comfort.

VAL. Did you steal wine bottles and use the money to buy a lottery ticket?

ESMERELDA. I just performed the penultimate role of my life, my swansong: Esmerelda Quipp, lunatic.

VAL. Court jester; we heard.

ESMERELDA. This is for you, Penny.

(ESMERELDA passes an envelope through the bars. PENNY rips it open and inside finds a cheque.)

VAL. You got a bank account!

PENNY. Is this for real?

ESMERELDA. It's your pension cheque. Now you can retire.

PENNY. It's a hundred freakin' grand!

ESMERELDA. Spend a little, save a lot. You'll need it in your dotage, trust me.

(H.B. enters and unlocks the cell door, leaving it open.)

H.B. Tea, Mrs. Quipp?

ESMERELDA. Lovely, thank you.

(H.B. exits.)

PENNY. What the f…?

ESMERELDA. Now, Miss Palermo; you've seen the worst of us. Go and assume your role. Do let us know when the film is released; jail birds' night out.

VAL. So you still think stage actors are superior to movie actors?

PENNY. Rosanna Palermo? I need a vodka…

ESMERELDA. Exactly what role are you researching?

PENNY. What the f…?

VAL. "Irma La Duce" the remake.

*(H.B. enters with **DOTTIE** in handcuffs.)*

PENNY. Class reunion.

VAL. Hi Dottie; what gives?

H.B. Five-finger discount, yet again.

ESMERELDA. But why do you keep doing this, Dottie? Your husband's rich.

DOTTIE. My husband's dead.

ESMERELDA. Oh dear, frightfully sorry.

PENNY. So, that means you're a rich widow, right?

DOTTIE. He was in debt up to his wazoo. I found out when the will was read. Now I'm broke.

VAL. How fast it can all change.

DOTTIE. I took a cue from Essie and I stole a diamond necklace, so now I have a place to live, I guess.

ESMERELDA. Officer, what is Mrs. Ramsbottom's bail set at?

H.B. Ten grand.

ESMERELDA. Do you accept cheques?

DOTTIE. You have a bank account?

ESMERELDA. Mildred kindly recommended her favourite financial institution and I managed to negotiate an account with no service charges, providing I leave a balance of fifty thousand in there.

(**DOTTIE** *faints;* **H.B.** *and* **VAL** *catch her;* **PENNY** *slaps her face.*)

PENNY. This is just so tempting…

(**DOTTIE** *comes to.*)

ESMERELDA. Won't be a moment. I'll just post your bail and then you can come live at Dolly's…Actually, it has a new name now: Welfarewell.

VAL. Nice place to visit, but…

ESMERELDA. Bite your tongue, Miss Palermo; you just never know.

DOTTIE. Rosanna Palermo?

(**DOTTIE** *faints.*)

ESMERELDA. "My poverty, but not my will, consents."

VAL. "I pay thy poverty, and not thy will."

PENNY. Romeo and freakin' Juliet. The end.

(*blackout*)

The End

ABOUT THE PLAYWRIGHT

PAMELA (CAT) DELANEY is a widely published journalist, humourist, and award-winning poet and playwright, a member of the Playwrights Guild of Canada, who also writes fiction, non-fiction satire, screenplays and web copy. An avid theatre-goer, wine aficionado, classical guitarist and badminton-player, she lives with several wicked, proofreading cats, a collie, who has an IQ higher than hers, and has a rather unique muse. A bit of a gypsy, Cat has always managed to find a home near the water, but she can't swim.

SCENE AND CHARACTER BREAKDOWNS

Act I, Scene 1 — Esmerelda's One-room Basement Flat
Open space, there could be a bed or just a pull-out chesterfield, a kitchen counter, maybe small appliances, an old fireplace (with mantel) on one wall where Merlin's bed and blanket are; (not too "old lady" a room; Esmerelda has some dignity left).

ESMERELDA only is in this scene.

Act I, Scene 2 — The Yard Outside Esmerelda's Flat
This can be set on the apron, or very far downstage and be created largely with illusion; it would help to have the image of a window at ground level; a garden shed might be a nice suggestive touch.

ESMERELDA and the **LANDLORD** are in this scene.

Act I, Scene 3 — The Night Desk in a Police Station
Pretty much H.B.'s office; we need a desk with drawers, computer, telephone, lots of papers and in-baskets, a chair for H.B. at the desk and one either across the desk or next to it for Esmerelda.

ESMERELDA, **H.B.** and **JENNIFER** are in this scene.

Act I, Scene 4 — The Front Desk of the Police Station
Just a high, stand-up registration desk (maybe it could double as a teller wicket in later scenes), and again, this can be done far downstage or on the apron.

ESMERELDA and **H.B.** are in this scene.

Act I, Scene 5 — A Bank
Basic accoutrements of banks, two teller wickets, a queue-up line that is roped with stanchions, and we need a security camera or two lodged high up, a police emergency call-button, plus the usual advertising posters about bank services (my favourites are the old Royal Bank of Canada one "Can Do!", which of course meant that half the people who applied for loans were not, in fact, told "can do", but "not a chance"; and the current one for The Bank of Nova Scotia that claims "You're Richer Than You Think" (haha-hahaha!)).

ESMERELDA, BANK TELLER #1, BANK TELLER #2 (LUCY), BANK CUSTOMER #1, and **MILDRED** are in this scene.

Act I, Scene 6 — The Holding Cell in the Police Station Jail
This is the most frequent setting in the play and must both incarcerate and expose the characters; there needs to be an operable door, and a bunch of bars, also a set of permanent cots (bunkbed style works best) and in the corner, with a drape that can be pulled around them, a sink and toilet, plus a couple of stools (pun intended) or plain chairs.

ESMERELDA, H.B., VAL, GLADYS, DOTTIE, PENNY, JENNIFER and **ALFRED** are in this scene.

Act I, Scene 7 — The Private Meeting Room
Just two chairs far downstage (so we can have the illusion of a walk down a corridor to get there from the previous scene), lit with spots will serve to show the austerity of this room, normally used to interrogate "real" criminals.

ESMERELDA and **ALFRED** are in this scene.

Act I, Scene 8 — The Holding Cell in the Police Station Jail
See Act I, Scene 6; same setting

ESMERELDA, H.B., VAL, GLADYS, DOTTIE, PENNY and **ALFRED** are in this scene.

Act II, Scene 1 — The Alleyway Behind a Restaurant
This would be kind of fun staged in an aisle in the house, but it can also be set on the apron or far downstage; we need a wall or area of shadows for Esmerelda to hide and the two bins (one for recycling and one for trash); simple. *Important note: glass will be broken in this scene and swept up by the Chef, so that needs to be considered when locating this scene.*

ESMERELDA and the **CHEF** are in this scene.

Act II, Scene 2 — Another Bank
We can use the same teller wickets as the previous bank, but need to dress this one up to be sure it shows as a different bank (maybe modernize the look).

ESMERELDA, BANK TELLER #3 and **MILDRED** are in this scene.

Act II, Scene 3 — The Holding Cell in the Police Station Jail
Same as previous.

ESMERELDA, VAL, PENNY, H.B., JENNIFER and **ALFRED** are in this scene.

Act III, Scene 4 — The Private Meeting Room
Same basic two chairs and stark light.

ESMERELDA and **ALFRED** are in this scene.

Act II, Scene 5 — The Holding Cell in the Police Station Jail
Same as previous.

ESMERELDA, VAL, PENNY, H.B., JENNIFER and **ALFRED** are in this scene.

Act II, Scene 6 — The Night Desk in a Police Station
Same as previous.

ALFRED, H.B. and **JENNIFER** are in this scene.

Act II, Scene 7 — A Courtroom
Classic courtroom with a judge's bench, the flag of the country positioned nearby, a witness stand, a long table with chairs where Esmerelda and Alfred sit, and seats for the witnesses and observers; keep it simple because this is where the comedy roars and we don't want the set to interfere.

ESMERELDA, JUDGE JULIUS, H.B., ALFRED, JENNIFER and **MILDRED** are in this scene.

Act II, Scene 8 — The Holding Cell in the Police Station Jail
Same as previous.

ESMERELDA, VAL, PENNY, H.B. and **DOTTIE** are in this scene.

PROPERTIES

(in no particular order)
A manual can-opener
A tin of cat food
A small dish and a spoon
A radio
Matches and candles
An older telephone (for **ESMERELDA**)
A slice of bread
A glass of water (clear glass)
Numerous bottles of prescription pills
A dead cat (black, please)
A cat basket and blanket
Two urns that contain ashes (alluded to only) of cats
A few plastic grocery store bags
A ratty old tea towel
A garden trowel
A garden spade
Two cellular telephones (for **LANDLORD** and **ALFRED**)
A cardboard cup of tea (take-away style)
A yellowing linen handkerchief (cotton will do)
A china teacup and saucer
A small carton of milk
A packet of biscuits/cookies
A telephone (at the police station)
A big green garbage bag
A coffee can
A five-dollar bill
Wool, knitting needles and some knitting
A two-part police form
Name tags for bank tellers (one must be "**LUCY**")
Paper money, including a "wad of bills"
A Starbuck's gift certificate
A robbery note
Handcuffs
Jail cell door keys
A pack of cigarettes and loose cigarettes
Sandwiches
Two bottles of spring water
A cup of black coffee
Written notes and reports (belonging to **ALFRED**)
Cots, pillows and blankets
A recycle bin
Several empty wine bottles

A dust pan and brush
A trash bin
A realistic-looking toy gun
A deck of playing cards
A portable stool
A clipboard, paper and pen (for **JENNIFER**)
Legal papers and a gavel (for **JUDGE JULIUS**)
A Bible
An envelope with a cheque in it

COSTUMES

ESMERELDA
(three outfits; two old ones, one new one)
Essentials: a walking cane; sensible shoes (but not sneaker-style); a carpetbag (think Mary Poppins); respectable stockings.

Act I, Scenes 1, 2, 3 and 4
Outfit #1: an old but clean dress (not floral!); a classic winter coat that is very old with a slightly tacky brooch; a shawl; perhaps a dignified, albeit older, hat; a pair of leather gloves, also worse for the wear.

Act I, Scenes 5, 6, 7 and 8, and Act II, Scenes 1, 2, 3, 4, 5, 6 and 7
Outfit #2: same as outfit #1, but a different dress (again, not floral!), perhaps with understated stripes.

Act II, Scene 8
Outfit #3: a brand new dress, perhaps a slightly brighter colour; new coat, hat, scarf and gloves; new shoes; and a really nice new brooch on the coat.

LANDLORD
(one outfit)

Act I, Scene 2
Outfit: jeans; shirt over a T-shirt, bomber jacket, sneakers or boots.

H.B.
(two outfits: one police uniform and one good suit for court)

Act I, Scenes 3, 4, 6 and 8, and Act II, Scenes 3, 6 and 8
Outfit #1: police uniform (the bottoms must be pants for contrast to the courtroom scene).

Act II, Scene 7
Outfit #2: a classy suit, the bottom of which is a skirt, and nice heels; we want good contrast to the tough cop image.

JENNIFER
(four outfits, all business-like, but not too stiff; as she feels the romance from **ALFRED**, she flowers a little)

Act I, Scene 3
Outfit #1: a pantsuit would work, with a simple blouse or top and flat shoes or low boots; she's not a sophisticated person, so nothing too hip and not much make-up.

Act I, Scenes 6 and 8
Outfit #2: a skirt, top and jacket with plain, low-heeled shoes.

Act II, Scenes 3 and 6
Outfit #3: dress pants and a nice top; maybe pant-boots.

Act II, Scene 7
Outfit #4: she's really dressed up in a dress and jacket for court, but the little added make-up, spiffy hair-do and glittery earrings tell us she's feeling romantic towards Alfred, and coming out of her shell a bit.

BANK CUSTOMER #1, BANK TELLERS #1, #2 and #3
Act I, Scene 5 and Act II, Scene 2
Any type of daytime/businessy attire is fine.

MILDRED
(three outfits, all of them upscale; she is not poor)
Act I, Scene 5
Outfit #1: a good coat over expensive boots, carrying a designer label handbag.

Act II, Scene 2
Outfit #2: a polished suit, gold jewelry, designer scarf and handbag, expensive shoes or boots.

Act II, Scene 7
Outfit #3: black dress with pearls and black patent leather pumps; maybe a hat, out of respect for being in court.

VAL/ROSANNA
(two outfits; she is practising to be Irma La Duce, round two, so she might take on the look of a French hooker in the second act when she is exposed)

Act I, Scenes 6 and 8
Outfit #1: red dress (tight fit), glittery shoes, lots of make-up and jewelry, maybe a faux-fur stole.

Act II, Scenes 3, 5 and 8
Outfit #2: tight black skirt, horizontal-striped top, red neckkerchief, high-heeled black pumps, lots of make-up and jewelry.

GLADYS
(one outfit, but it must correspond to Esmerelda's remark: lots of white, including the hair-do)

Act I, Scenes 6 and **8**
Outfit: white skirt and jacket, white top or blouse; maybe silver pumps and silver handbag (the "woman from Glad")

DOTTIE
(two outfits; she is a bit of a wreck, so her clothes and hair should be, too)

Act I, Scenes 6 and **8**
Outfit #1: messy hair, baggy jeans, floral T-shirt, sneakers (decidedly un-sexy).

Act II, Scene 8
Outfit #2: perhaps corduroy pants, an old flannel shirt, sneakers (again, not sexy; we have work to do on this woman); or, we could put her in widow's weeds for this scene.

PENNY
(one outfit suitable for an experienced hooker, trying to look a bit younger than she is)

Act I, Scenes 6 and **8**, and **Act II, Scenes 3, 5** and **8**
Outfit: given that she's been working the streets and drinking when she is hauled into jailed in her first scene, we need her to look the part; remember, she's a pro and would not resort to stereotypical anything.

ALFRED
(three outfits: three different suits, shirts, ties and pairs of shoes)
Essentials: briefcase; maybe spectacles.

Act I, Scenes 6, 7 and **8**
Outfit #1: a shirt, tie, suit, good shoes.

Act II, Scenes 3, 4, 5 and **6**
Outfit #2: a different shirt, tie, suit and shoes.

Act II, Scene 7
Outfit #3: his best suit, shirt, tie and shoes; or a lawyer's robes.

JUDGE JULIUS
(one outfit)

Act II, Scene 7
Outfit: a judge's robes, but we want her to retain some level of feminine style, so maybe great earrings or a big bracelet (like a gold cuff, perhaps), and her hair is perfect, as well as her make-up; she's a class act.

AUDIO EFFECTS

Act I
Scene 1: sound effects on the radio (drums, soldiers marching)
Scene 3: a telephone rings
Scene 5: police sirens in the distance
Scene 6: the blast of a coffee truck's horn; the flushing of a toilet
Scene 7: the ring of a cellular telephone (twice)

Act II
Scene 1: a caterwaul
Scene 2: police sirens in the distance

PREVIOUS WINNERS OF THE CANADIAN PLAYWRIGHTS CONTEST AVAILABLE FROM SAMUEL FRENCH

$38,000 FOR A FRIENDLY FACE
by Kristin Shepherd

BINGO BABES
by Isabel Duarte

CLOSURE
by Ron Blicq

KITCHEN WITCHES
by Caroline Smith

MAPLE LODGE
by Colleen Curran

SHADOWS ON OAK ISLAND
by Garnet Hirst with Deborah L. Preeper

THAT DARN PLOT
by David Belke

YEAR IN THE DEATH OF EDDIE JESTER
by T. Gregory Argall

Breinigsville, PA USA
23 August 2010
244011BV00004B/2/P

The American Poetry Series

Books by Dennis Schmitz

We Weep for Our Strangeness
Double Exposures
Goodwill, Inc.
String

Singing

Dennis Schmitz

The Ecco Press
New York

Library of Congress Cataloging in Publication Data
Schmitz, Dennis, 1937–   /Singing.
(The American Poetry Series, Vol. 31)
I. Title.   II. Series
PS3569.C517S5   1985   811.54   84-13641
ISBN 0-88001-068-1

FIRST EDITION

Grateful acknowledgment is made to the following
magazines in which these poems first appeared:

Antaeus: "Singing," "Skinning-the-Cat," "Country Deaths,"
      "Lucky Tiger," "1942"

Columbia: "Building on Farmer Creek"

Field: "A Picture of Okinawa," "Uncle," "On a Dark Afternoon,"
      "Stung," "Cutting Out a Dress," "A Man & a Woman,"
      "A Letter to Ron Silliman on the Back of a Map of the Solar System,"
      "Attic," "Strays"

Iowa Review: "Dressing Game," "The History of Armor," "Coma"

Ironwood: "Kindergarten," "Apostle to the Birds," "The Coal Bin
      Imagined from My Grandmother's Description"

Tendril: "Finding the Way," "Sabotage (Part I)," "Marriage"

Tri-Quarterly: "The Knot," "News," "Gill Boy"

For Gerry, Judy, Kathy, Jean

Contents

III

I

Singing

In grandma's nap the victrola skips
to Mimi's consumptive solo.
    Eighty-five, angina

pectoris crushing
her chest into the sheets,
she sings the thick Victor 78's

to herself, sings a husband
back, the horse's bite still smudged
blue above his collarbone
    where she would put her own lips

down, moaning.
    Only five, I leaned the door
closed & watched
her face shape over the unheard
while my mother called through

    the house below
that lemonade was with the others.
I won't answer,

I won't come back easily
from the close room, the only light
thrashed through a catalpa
branch as my cousins swing out

into July dark
defiant & greedy for pain.
    I am youngest of the youngest
daughter, Eve, who had neither voice

     nor moral sweetness.
I sing faintly
     in tune with the sleepers,
awed that no words
lie so well as the implied
melody we keep

in rhythm with our dead.

A Picture of Okinawa

Out of adult hearing
the birds stammer this place
the animals intact
the remembered trees mismade
because a child painted them

from radio news & the interdicted
marsh back of Catfish Slough—
no GI drab but the Rousseau greens
snakes shed in their turnings

from heaven-held aquas & cerulean.
When the last Japanese soldier
gave up thirty years late
crashed down in some islander's

backyard, the sniper webbings cradling
his navel to the bandoliers
& commando knife with the four
metal knuckle-rings, I still looked
for my soldier uncle in this picture

my aunt never sent
to show how I imagined the enemy
condemned to eat close to heaven
the lonely madness for another's flesh,
his greenish waste wrapped in leaves

& stabbed on treeforks,
the mottled arm reaching for birds,
leaf by leaf making himself
innocent of his weapons—
only thirty years to come down human.

5

Kindergarten

Bee-logic: each small life
for the hive,
but not one of them lived out

at the same speed—
your heart thuds *fortissimo* but slow,
my heart trots to its death.

Proto-druggist pickpocket or priest
begin as mysteries to themselves.
Big-Head Vincent who chews his pastels

& wipes spit with the blue
over his squat trees,
& Levonn too who wets himself

is one of us.
Our keeper Sister Agnes,
wrinkled as a peach-nut & left-handed,

sings Latin, whose inside
is God's, she says, but we can go in
too with our tongues & the head

will follow, simplifying
heaven. Vincent went to heaven
in wet April. We sang a few words

of "Nunc Dimittis" among the gladiolus
& floribunda wreaths,
gripping each other's fingers

as we knelt all points in a compass,
expecting somehow to sing
Vincent up. But we belonged

to the headless Vincent
someone crayoned on the cloakroom
wall under his coathook,

the feet broken
right-angles, the heavy
arms straining against gravity—

a child's unfinished body,
waxy & insistent.

Skinning-the-Cat

& this is the organ which was made last
I said, nine years old & proud
to go back & forth with the pan brimming

from my aunt's kitchen into the dark.
Because sight is burned out,
the hand-linked adults around the dining
room table overload the other senses

sharing distaste, afraid of the future.
My grandmother passes from her wet hands
into my mother's something slippery

with unknown fluid.
I am too young to play the WW II games
they did when electricity was uncertain

or during lights-out practice drills,
so I am chosen to carry
these common objects felt in common

turned by dark & suggestion
into an animal's insides: cantaloupe waste
slimy with seeds, a few grapes heated . . .

to this day I don't recall
what stood for which organ, the quivering
unborn, the one like a prickly
tree-gall. The not-dead groaning

of the party-goers keeps on
as they feel individually & pass on
the perfect animal the group animal.

Uncle

The smell is laid down—
even the jays who will not light

bring it on their feathers.
They fight overhead for room;

their fuzz comes down
in fennel & ryegrass.

Smell on your wife when she undresses.
Sniff the fish knife in camp surgery

where man cuts out the hook.
& go down on all fours,

mortal, strapped to a colostomy sack,
a separate gravity you squeeze

between your legs, pound
until it bursts on the tent floor.

Aunt Frannie is calling your pet name
in the woods where you broke

the expensive Fenwick rod,
yards of flyline looping over manzanita

toward heaven. Your pups,
their backs broken with a spade,

snort from the highway ditch,
still domestic.

But the smell the raccoon dug at,
snout speckled with egg,

trapped by willfulness
in the garbage drum he overturned,

is rage.

On a Dark Afternoon

grandma's fingers peck
the moiré birds bleeding in a tree-
of-heaven pattern.
She patches the opposed lovers

on either side of the spread—
& a third, a fetal, thumb-sized
version of herself, lies down

between them who were her parents.
Memory makes them blue,
& the hands they reach out

to join, a mauve around the apple
with one crescent bite
creating the notion of fault.

There she sews her name
who illustrates their fall,
in bed herself with her work—
her invalid's sheets

iridescent with Oxydol & blueing.
A thousand rootlets
of thread go down into the ivy
which smothers her left

withered hand.
Inside that hand a creeper squirms
through red sumac:
autumn has leaves trailing down

its back.
It thrashes under her stiffened fingers.
It wants to crawl up inside her
& sleep.

Stung

to anger, a kind of species outrage,
I cursed & vowed to go back
at night when the wasps would cluster,
knot & re-knot into entropy.
Now I am alone

between the barn & the implement shed
for a long while looking up
but concentrating my polarity down here
feeling the planet turn

against human weight
its incredible friction showering off stars
which are the only other light

until just inside the shed I set fire
to a rag wet with cooking oil
I've wired to a long pole: it smoulders

then flares when I wave it
into webs as I inch the pole high
to the corner nest

iridescent with wings.
It's hard to do what the eye tells us—
coordinate the distant

fire as the long pole flexes
off bits of burning rag or bodies
(I can't distinguish)

& they fall among machinery,
illumine, close up, levers
& gears, a greasy differential
set down between sawhorses.

Dressing Game

After the men hunt,
the woman cleans the game.
She follows the puckered skin with a match
to burn off pinfeathers,
pushes & kneads squirrels from their hides,
printing against a haunch,

against the suddenly revealed
scraped breastbone, her live flesh.
Over the oiled underskin
her fingermarks, her scars,
the thick crown of a wart,

maybe a hair between her flesh & theirs.
The knife-nick will be cooked in,
the touches-for-nothing.
Even the trash organs

pick up her image as she sorts,
breaking the membranes, turning the joints
180 degrees to break their lock
on remembered fields,
burrows & slide-holes in burdock.

Afterward she soaks in the stream—
the red curling off,
the current clotting around rocks.
She lets her soiled shirt fill,

removes it & wrings it. & her pants
as she swings them,
emptied of herself, fill too with a clear
though invisible body
which passes, shivering the denim, back
into the stream.

The Knot

Better for us to rise out of the sweaty
sacking two bodies;
better for love to falter,
to be subtracted to oneself—

& hours later, still inventing
the vernacular kiss,
wade the loft hay looking

for the plain gold ring which bound us,
pressed down by our struggling
to the mouths of the animals

nourished from above as we are:
chaff, ratshit, apotheosis—
holding back because which taste

is the one we most desire?
On all fours going
down I comb hay, gunnysacks

& unwrinkle the shirt in which you knotted
watch & ring to keep them.
Hay-must coats my back; the fine hairs
in my nose thicken as I breathe it.
Below, in the horse-boxes, you whinny.

Country Deaths

turned on the endless wheel of creatures

Blood is mixed with oil
stink on County Double-A to lay the dust
to patch a flesh neither dirt nor meat
until God put his finger in

each hole & said let man come forth
& learn to live with his instincts
coupled to a modified '64 Chevy,
the Falstaff empties

rolling to the back seat.
Let him buck
the cream & red Harley
through shucked corn at 3 a.m.
screaming joy & reflexive defiance,

insects & studs punched onto his leathers.
Pheasants bloom in the headlamp,
but he must reject them.
He will live commanded
by faulty sensibility, one fuse

shorted, one precious connection.
& some night rattle in sumac through
to the slough, his elbows shattered against
saplings, eyes smeared
as branches whip back
a vision of universal circuitry.

If he must he goes down
a third time inhaling leeches,
weeds, & the fruit hulls opened
        by a ski-boat prop;
or if not worthy, not animal enough—

unable to die,
        he can come back
to count his own fingers
crushed into an Aeromotor's rusty gears

or be wrecked by his own contrivance
high on the platform warped
forty years but still preserved by oil

        sprayed from worn bearings.
The oil scent changes
direction with the wind as it burns
in dry July storms,

the vane tip sawing smudge & blue.
This time the vanes are locked behind him;
the wind instead carries his blood
        down thirty feet onto the row crop
spokes connected to an illusive point
on the horizon.

Building on Farmer Creek

to Tom Crawford

A stream sweetened by roots,
    the sun in two buckets
you lug back
to us your arms counterstressed

with fatigue. The mix is blended
until the sky tires & the blue

    cement thickens,
beads as its weight sweats out water.
Man or wooly lumber oozing musk,
knot for knot ennobled
by unwitnessed existence that presses

for form against us—
the footings are poured before you can wonder,

the aggregate stirred
with the same shovel Gary earlier laid
in the coals to cook biscuits.
You quit a dull but honorable job to live here;
looking down, you see mud to blind yourself,
burned-back grass,
& the shit of the animals you love—

let them multiply, let them feed us.
The goats pluck sour grass
outside the arbitrary limits of the chalkline.
We are not exhausted.
We race the dogs beyond our strength

until I sit by you, your credulous friend,
my nerves retreating under blisters.
I want one of the three houses you plan—
I will choose a work for which I am not fit.
The stream runs on.
The three of us sit down in it still clothed.

Cutting Out a Dress

Sara's fingers will find the way
before her eyes do
in the river of print-goods daubed

with human figures.
At thirteen she lays out
a world to fit her imagined body
in the attic room held
by its yellow light high in the treetops.
Every night she sheds into the outside

animals her childhood taught:
no panda nor hippogriff,
but Jake our setter run down by a car,
a snail popped underfoot,
a sluggish fly tapping
out its life between two panes—

each death a kind of rhythmic moulting,
a forgiven pain
her scissors briefly isolates.
In the bedroom below, my wife
& I each think we wrestle
a different angel as we shake

& pant in an unbreakable marriage-hold.
The floor above us trembles—
the sewing machine
thumping the same cloth over & over.
The pulse is threaded

into the arm-linked humans
repeated to infinity—
a life so simple its seamless embrace
could be skin itself.

II

A Man & a Woman

A man & a woman both held by her wings:
she flaps the wings & lice shake out,
ping off the tin roof.
Below them the farmer's mongrel yips

into a sky defined by orchard rows.
Lost in jubilance, the dog rolls & irregularly
twists up two-legged at the sight.
But the woman is crossed

with wires; the red-coated metal pulls
welts under her breasts,
divides to quivering hemispheres

the belly, pendulous, waxy with sweat.
Overhead they go in her agony,
from the ground an almost human coupling.
Skimming the limber April growth,

snagging open cuts,
they mew & snort in pain.
The wires move as she tries harder—
from the pubis one wire

comes out a rust point that won't callus.
How she hates her strength,
how she longs for heaven.

Finding the Way

Over the inland level suburbs
a drive-in movie
screen: the giant female insect is rising

from Los Angeles her eggs pouring from a wound
down to the tract houses—
medicinal neons purify the hatch
in the next frame

as we round a curve before the Sunrise exit,
the tight Japanese car with five people
arguing the disaster

is really a failure of allegory,
resignation, or even loss of scale.
The chimneys webbed shut,
stucco specked with muculent larval debris.
One householder using a rake-

handle pokes clear the window so he can look
back in at his family—
the three men refuse to say more.
My sister drives with the map,
blue for water, red & black lines
for the streets of Folsom, sloping across
her thighs.

The History of Armor

Gilles de Rais, so-called Bluebeard,
not called but occupied
by voices he cut from children at Black Mass,
does he seem our ancestor because he sacrificed

children, did the unspeakable,
a joy so involved that his silence echoed
his general Jeanne d'Arc who would not repeat
unto madness the order of heaven

that made her wear man's clothes?
A grown man doubled his weight—
he blistered, then callused over at every joint

for the sake of his armor.
Women had no such protection.
The previous age's plague still clung—
field after field, sorghum & low wheat
rusted; a contradiction of weeds

bore down the riprap
granary walls. The thin women ate
their way out of the sour grain
till they were soured, their skirts pulled
back winters to show fur & cloth

leggings. The Church forgives them;
the amputees & deserters
they gave birth to never forgave them.

Apostle to the Birds

The halo behind the Last Supper,
the cracks in the plaster around Judas's throat
as the halo tightens:
to choke or to fly, who can tell

until an arm lifts itself,
& the forearm begins to feather; the wrist,

pimpled & oily, flaps into eternity.
Out of the squat light
which substitutes for gravity
in the picture, Judas goes up, relieved—

no angel, but a common suicide
who leaves this world sobbing, coatless.
How do you receive him
who wanted to fly so much he fasted

with Jesus, so much that as a boy he lay down
with the hens in his parents' brood-house
sticky with flyspeck & feed,
so much that he practiced his death-kick

even before the painter saw him
as a talent to be exploited?

A Letter to Ron Silliman on the Back of a Map of the Solar System

I weigh 486 lbs on Jupiter
   I can't tell you why
I am crying why
          whole ridges of the memory
pull loose this immense gravity
keeps us down
under the slide I discarded first
   my old father who weighed more
here on my back a smaller hump somehow
my penis came out
   wrong or a strangely distended
heart girls touch for luck I threw
   down my weapons too what use
I said poor Aeneas is the afternoon
when distance turns our atmosphere
to frozen gas & shadows the gods give
         a discernible half-life
winks by the best
of our instruments the father
Jupiter ate the most promising
   of his children the Latin myths say

little they were not grateful
to the sly Greeks a fallen
   city was given curiously foreign
buildings with supports constructed
   on heavenly principles Cassandra
for instance screamed & the water-clocks
ran faster in our color bands
   sodium insects & our smaller
life take on a radiance &
become explosive when it rains we know
it is a warning

31

do not even cry the atmosphere
is unstable keep it under sawdust wet
with oil the moist armpits & loins
    are unstable for our use only
the subtle dust that drifts
    down when the last of the fallen memory
settles & Jupiter surrenders
a final disguise for our mothers
    were raped & we grow up half-gods in turn
to eat or forget our real origins

Sabotage

expresses the self you'd rather spoil
than give, a forfeit,
to the enemy—or even to a brother,
who might say, as mine did: *kneel,*

I want to see polish on yr lips.
I remember bobbing to kiss
his sneakers which I had polished

as a joke for a cousin's wedding.
I was eleven, but now
foot-fetish is a term I associate
with whitey's arrogance to play blackface,

or with subordination of desire,
wanting to kill, but instead
incorporating the enemy
in a literal sense like the cannibal arachnid

wrapping its misinterpreted young.
For years I wanted a gothic revenge
like the one I imagined
for the black shoeshine jockey at the Randolph
subway stop. Mid-sleep, my head vibrating

against the window of a late night local,
I thought the black man's power
when he went down on his knees

to polish, caress, rub his spit
into the stranger's shoe.
I imagined him
humming to it under the storefront neon.
The shoe would go up near his mouth.
He dropped, dribbled all he'd held back,

caught it again
in the blackening, scrubbed it to liquid,
with his palm worked
the leather, skin to skin, feeling

how the human welt followed the shoe welt.
With one finger he kept the pulse
moving, going up the man's leg—
the color climbed with his hand,

the polish darkening the other's skin
past the sock edge up,
shining the light hairs
until the stranger flesh was like his—
soft, the whole body dozing
in symbiotic rhythm with his, darker,
the sheen & sweat even coating an insect

which closed like a knot in one polished eyefold.

II

Other brothers fight. My own sons so knotted into
complementary musculature that their quarrel—
who'll feed our ratty chickens—becomes a problem
in geometry. Until the older hurts the boy who's
crying now. I splash all the water from the bucket
on them.

& explain how not to fight. Explain Konrad
Lorenz's gander Paulsen: say chickens fight or don't
fight the same way. They won't let themselves kill;
they sabotage their own urges in rapid, stochastic
penance. Beak wide and ruffed larger, the dominant
one interrupts itself mid-charge to chase an imagined
enemy to the side of the weaker one. Or the weaker
pretends to feed or be distracted by something,
something it won't eat mixed in the shit & fallen
food. It will not fight, but it knows only this way
to submit.

Karl, our Chicago friend, for example, who lay his
head near a D-8 tread to stop the construction at
Diablo Canyon. If the slowed machine had gone on,
the friable clay tread castoffs dropping as the
machine shuttered, stopped several head-widths
away? The red-faced driver screaming: if he would
have had a Goya beak & the goggle-eyed Goya
owlishness of *¿No hay quien nos desate?*, who
would've withstood his attack?

Karl called it *liability*, the Christian peace a man
gives his enemy when he excuses the belligerent
from a death that won't hold them both.

Protesting the death penalty as he had protested the
ITT in Chile, the draft and Nixon's Cambodia
because guilt is indivisible no matter how many
dead, Karl walked eight days to the state capital
carrying a ½-scale electric chair, strapped to himself
a weight he couldn't put down to enter a car. By the
time he got to the vigil, it was a cat's-cradle of
2×2's & wire, a device, a conductor of rage. Cars
ran him into the roadside weeds, the splintered
colonizing bindweed, the troubled fire, pyracantha,
whose berries draw small birds to the thorns. Was
he the fool I called him? Were the few dozen people
who went into his campaign, walked with him in
relays, his fools? We were so embarrassed we didn't
pledge. I quarreled with my wife three days, & so
we didn't drive to meet him at the first overnight
farm town. We didn't walk. Was his a displacement
activity? The sideways walk, the cramped stasis I see
in the boys' wrestling, the one's blood melting into
the chaff & rice-hulls a single foolish hen pecks at
between their shoes?

Coma

Done with myself, I asked
to lie down with the stroke victims,
to be one with those who keep themselves
in being by concentration—
the war-deaths who wake in a civilian eternity,

the army re-ups, the cancer-sufferers
who adore their own dying,
for whom the fear of living again

blurs the fear of death:
a fatigue not with pain, but with habit.
Already I've practice-slept

the Vietnam War through—
if My-Lai happens it happens in this unrelieved
dreaming that blooms white-haired

out of the brainlight traced on the monitor
by my bed—an aging the technician
waits for before he calls the White House

& Mr. Truman answers that
he remembers me as a boy spread
sleeping across a pew, tired of the Lord

who let the Chinese cross the Yalu.
My wife has grown older
by the same relentless science that keeps her

awake. Why can't I die
of this blindness rusted into my head?
What I once saw I saw unable to be moved,

a scapegoat, a second-born—
in group therapy the last one to answer,
to make a memory. Only the prosthetic

heroes can will to pick up
this world—sweating, they flail, they tap,
they pinch for it as it rolls

out of the therapist's hands, very small.

News

The *Chronicle* "Green Sheet" dries out
BIC pen mustaches & goggles,
underwear women
the boys decorated with paisley lesions,

interpreting the news.
Extinction seems a protracted, ironic task:
though Hitler's
manager Albert Speer dies

only a few pages ago,
I remember Hitler's death
on the radio was the work of an age,

a whole industry;
Eva Braun was anyone's sister gone wrong.
Finally I go on my belly
with the children to highlight

what is real. Newsprint bruises
ripple all over me;
faces come off on my sleeves

as I sweat & fill
page after page, call for new stacks.
Captions pull off like scabs,

but reversed:
this news understood only in mirrors,
accepted by the body,

will teach me shame.
My wife kneels too
on what we once thought important:

boldface sex crimes,
ferocious nations & burned-down discos.
Unaware of all they carry,

both boys stagger
in with old *Trib* issues,
the *Guardian, The Berkeley Barbs*

so yellow from garage weather
that they flake & snow
down on us lost, unrecoverable lives.

III

The Coal Bin Imagined from
My Grandmother's Description

as she gives me the scuttle
& snaps the light cord at the top of the stairs,
means it is so far down that I must fall

headfirst, which I do,
my aim, until I reach this remote earth,
taken from stories children agree to,

wanting ghastly secrets.
But the beasts that happened after my words
to make them were only the kind of horse
or dog a fat first-grade pencil draws,
hardly able to manage their own gravity—

their eyes, dots heavy from lifting blackness.
& so I discover what coal is, how slow—
I pick up a lump & think I feel fronds,
or a paw-print pressing back

my own blackened hand.
I go into the room-sized bin—
here I build a campfire
to begin to make the way back.
The first step is to re-invent everything,

to domesticate what I imagined,
to bring light out of all that scribble.
But the weight of the dark

flattened cups & a canteen almost half-gone,
flattened even my pockets.
The horses couldn't breathe.
They knelt & rolled until their curves

43

gave out against one another.
I looked into the eyes of one dog
& saw his black vision go dense

from the inside,
the pupils of his eyes mold
over my face reflected backwards,
that crooked grin knotted over my thumb

as I sucked comfort & cried.
It took years to give up questions,
to let the species go crippled.
Now at last I'm almost happy
with the blackness though I still live

with you, poor horses caught in implication—
if only I had an eraser to rub over
your fuzzy muzzles,
if only I could wipe the black-flecked drool.

Gill Boy

for John, my son

The toys I bought for you
splash down in your brothers' tub,
are rubbed paintless,
protean, in the 15 yrs coming down:

the space vehicle Apollo,
the rubbery aliens,
& the tooth-scarred astronaut
who trails air-hose,
prepared to go breathless

into the child's world.
You lived only five days,
unable to surface, cyanotic

in the isolette, then cold—
the way I've learned to accept you
when I wash your two brothers real,
when I shape each

of their small parts over
& over again with soap.
I tried to forget, to sublimate,
but under seven inches of bathwater,
out of reach,

you learned to breathe.
The suds your brothers leave,
the soapy waste

webs galls & scaly eyelets
all over your skin
so cruel no one could love you

& want to survive.

Marriage

At 5 a.m. a man crawls; his wife rolls over
hauling the moonlit bedclothes
(this is savor & praise)—

    the half-heard
cedar waxwing, the burr riding
a pants leg to what
oblivion: all come to only after
       mixing, dilution or breakdown—
the ache is not the kind a tongue says.

    Our dog, like me, has no grace:
the cat his sulky plaything flops, refuses
by gritting teeth against the geranium

tub. Its teethmarks would be full
of blood, but its guilt
      keeps pain a negotiable

restraint. You are shaky all day,
      presupposing desire.
When I open the kitchen door
you burn your hand against the stove,

sizzle of thumb touched
down, a perfume rusted into flesh.

Attic

Mice, their eyes studded
by a 40-W bulb

or barn swallows spread out against
one small hole, tearing

themselves to get in.
I'm belly-down on splintery board

without a shirt, balancing over rafters.
Sometimes up to my wrists in cellulose

& rat-dirt, I touch *National
Geographics* or the cardboard violin-case

webbed to 2×10's, scrape the bloodied
overhead where I have to writhe

to get under while my wife
below, the ceiling plaster sounding

between us, syncopates then redoes Chopin's
Black-Key Étude. I change

hands when she does, sweating
at the *forte;* in tandem we release

one hold for the next
in my secret crawl to the cupola.

Every time I see more as I stand,
the cupola's shutters one by one

ascending my face until my eyes
are clear: a kind of helmet

I grow into, the outside laddered,
inimical. The music rippling through me.

Strays

     Long after the bee dies
the sting melts in the wound:
1961, impatient Anne,
our firstborn, teething on bagels—
you took up her cry
     denying nothing,

even dawn could not come
between you in your common song.
I heard you
800 miles away when I called

collect to tell you this story
I couldn't end
with the irony which would let me
come back shaking chiggers out of my clothes,
shower with you,
unafraid to eat dirt, the last darkness,
under the nails as I claw

two baloney sandwiches & an apple
southwest of Kearney,
the one road flexing with heat-pools.
From horizon to horizon

the eye never touches down.
My only ride in five hrs
comes at a one-pump truck stop—
a drug co. pickup delivering lab animals.
The driver in fatigue blues has me sit
with them, share
cages, rather crates of voiceless strays,
their vocal cords cut, he says,

so they will not rouse or confuse
one another.
After he has coffee & I try to call,
I wedge myself between tailgate & crates,
legs around pack & down-bag,

my arms free for tenderness.
As we shake & sway into the curves,
I poke between the cage slats,
let one mongrel gum my fingers—
it's love-hunger: his milk teeth won't break skin.
I have nothing to give him

that is not my own discontent,
that is not this plunge over a dirt track

to the driver's white clapboard house,
improbable, neat, in a stand of poplars.
Halfway across the yard
his wife meets him with some forgotten papers.

Suspicious but overpowered,
she will not look at me
because the thing is compounded by my fright.
The driver will not notice
the trill of insects (it is evening),
the grinding tires,
as he horses the truck around in gravel.

Lucky Tiger

The driver counts us
by twos, the gloomy with the prescient,
    fat by thin: not one
wants to see out.
They want to push their legs straight,

    try a near body fit
to the stranger, rock
away as the bus downshifts to turn
out of the area of boarded stores,

massage parlors where the implied
    corrects the real.
My handkerchief is spread
over the greasy seatback,
    over the correlative
odor of pomander

orange in my aunt's closet,
    its acid dissolving
the sweaty darkness where I hid
as I hide now
deliberate in pretend sleep
    my face turned
to a world distorted by another greasy

headprint on the window.
I slept & the same years slept
    secret, scratched.
From the closet I barely hear
my older, slow cousin corrected, his hand
    I sense guided—
chew this bread he says to himself

chew, & as I knew he would, rubs
        the greasy part in his hair
before he molds the sticky approximates,
alphabetical animals I who already knew
        how to read taught him.
Bite Denny he told the animal he rubbed

        near my mouth.
This still stands for that:
        his urine smell, the Lucky Tiger
my aunt stroked into his hair,
her hand shining from the contact
with him, her voice
        implying love.

1942

Treelevel night, innocent of planes—
hot night, mildewed
Iowa dawn a few hours above the porch.
Down by the slough something snaps

through brush or eats,
snout down in fur & loose matter.
I want to come back to the *Photoplays*
& mystery novels rotting

inside the cottage's sawndown chiffonier,
the summers-only smells,
involve every sense in what I was—
not caring whether I am
predator or the one fed on,
but connected as they are by a chemical reaction,
make the dark crawl

to the watering place,
that one undefinable sense
singing in vibration with the other's pulse.
I can bring back the Chicago dance-band,

the Philco's indicator more red
as the sound grows
& is cut mid-song by louder war-news.
When I concentrate I can feel
the slippery 12-gauge as I sweat against its stock,
waiting for birds;
I can bring back the smell

of my father's
long-johns knotted on a towel-bar,
the tick of the midges
burned up in the Coleman lamp,
celestial, short-range lives whirled by the heat
of mistaken desire—
but I can't bring back all the senses at once,

not even one body entire:
one midge, nor anything as big as
my younger sister sweating out fever,
her hair caught in a bunk spring

as she thrashes to escape
whatever predator doubles her body heat.
The night she died I lay on the bunk above,
trying to draw in the music,
dilate with the radio's ruby eye,
my mouth forming as the doctor

cooed instructions to her,
& then to my parents to take me
to their room where I lay in what I could
remember of her position
& exhaled the longheld remainder of her song.

A Note About the Author

Dennis Schmitz was born in Dubuque, Iowa, and educated at Loras College and the University of Chicago. He teaches at California State University, Sacramento.

Schmitz has received grants from the National Endowment for the Arts and the Guggenheim Foundation.